the new
VEGETARIAN
cookbook

the new
VEGETARIAN
cookbook

Roz Denny

HERMES
HOUSE

This edition first published in 1998 by Hermes House
27 West 20th Street, New York, NY 10011

HERMES HOUSE books are available for bulk purchase for sales promotion
and for premium use. For details, write or call the sales director,
Hermes House, 27 West 20th Street, New York, NY 10011;
(800) 354-9657

Hermes House is an imprint of
Anness Publishing Limited

ISBN 1 84038 074 8

Publisher: Joanna Lorenz
Project Editor: Jack Straw
Designer: Adrian Morris
Photographer: Michael Michaels
Home Economist: Wendy Lee

Printed and bound in Singapore by Star Standard Industries Pte. Ltd.

1 3 5 7 9 10 8 6 4 2

NOTE: Some vegetarians may prefer not to use
Worcestershire sauce in cooking, in which case
mushroom ketchup is an excellent substitute.
Anchovy essence may be omitted from recipes.

THE LEAF SYMBOL NEXT TO A RECIPE INDICATES THAT IT IS SUITABLE FOR VEGANS

CONTENTS

SOUPS
&
STARTERS

Tantalizing appetizers range from traditional favorites – including
soups that could be served either before a main course or on their own
as a light and wholesome meal – to more exotic dishes for elegant dinners.

Vegetable Stock

Use this versatile stock as the basis for all good soups and sauces. If you have an extra large saucepan, or stock pot, why not make double the quantity and freeze several batches?

MAKES 10 CUPS
2 leeks, roughly chopped
3 stalks celery, roughly chopped
1 large onion, with skin, chopped
2 pieces fresh ginger root, chopped
3 garlic cloves, unpeeled
1 yellow pepper, seeded and chopped
1 parsnip, chopped
mushroom stems
tomato peelings
3 tbsp light soy sauce
3 bay leaves
bundle of parsley stalks
3 sprigs of fresh thyme
1 sprig of fresh rosemary
2 tsp salt
ground black pepper
15 cups cold water

1 Put all the ingredients into a very large saucepan or a stock pot.

2 Bring slowly to a boil, then lower the heat and simmer for 30 minutes, stirring from time to time.

3 Allow the liquid and vegetables to cool. Strain, discard the vegetables and the stock is ready to use. Alternatively, chill or freeze the stock and keep it to use as required.

CRISP CROÛTONS

Easy to make and simple to store, these croûtons add a delightful touch to fresh home made soups.

They are also an ideal way of using up stale bread. Speciality bread such as Ciabatta or baguettes can be thinly sliced to make the nicest, crunchiest croûtons, but everyday sliced loaves can be cut into interesting shapes for fun entertaining. Use a good quality, flavorless oil such as sunflower or groundnut, or for a fuller flavor brush with extra virgin olive oil. Alternatively, you could use a flavored oil such as one with garlic and herbs or chilli.

Preheat the oven to 400°F. Place the croûtons on a baking sheet, brush with your chosen oil than bake for about 15 minutes until golden and crisp. They crisp up further as they cool. Store them in an airtight container for up to a week. Reheat in a warm oven if liked, before serving.

Sweetcorn and Potato Chowder

This creamy, hearty and substantial soup is high in both fiber and flavor. It's wonderful served with thick crusty bread and topped with some melted Cheddar cheese.

SERVES 4
1 onion, chopped
1 garlic clove, crushed
1 medium size potato, chopped
2 stalks celery, sliced
1 small green pepper, seeded, halved and sliced
2 tbsp sunflower oil
2 tbsp butter
2½ cups stock or water
salt and ground black pepper
1¼ cups milk
1 × 7 oz can lima beans
1 × 11 oz can corn kernels
good pinch dried sage

1 Put the onion, garlic, potato, celery and green pepper into a large saucepan with the oil and butter.

2 Heat the ingredients until sizzling then turn the heat down to low. Cover and sweat the vegetables gently for 10 minutes, shaking the pan occasionally.

3 Pour in the stock or water, season to taste and bring to a boil. Turn down the heat, cover and simmer gently for about 15 minutes.

4 Add the milk, beans and corn – including their liquors – and the sage. Simmer again for 5 minutes. Check the seasoning and serve hot.

Triple Red Soup 🍂

Vibrant in color and taste, this soup is quickly made. Use a red onion – if you can find one – it will enhance the final appearance.

SERVES 4–6
1 red pepper, seeded and chopped
1 onion, chopped
1 garlic clove, crushed
2 tbsp olive oil
1 × 14 oz can chopped tomatoes
4 cups stock
2 tbsp long grain rice
2 tbsp Worcestershire sauce
1 × 7 oz can red kidney beans
1 tsp dried oregano
1 tsp sugar
salt and ground black pepper
fresh parsley, chopped, and Cheddar
  cheese, grated, to garnish

1 Put the pepper, onion, garlic and oil into a large saucepan. Heat until sizzling then turn down to low. Cover and cook gently for 5 minutes.

2 Add the rest of the ingredients, except the garnishes, and bring to a boil. Stir well, then simmer – covered – for 15 minutes. Check the seasoning, garnish and serve hot. Omit the Cheddar cheese for a vegan soup.

Chinese Tofu and Lettuce Soup 🍂

This light, clear soup is brimming with nourishing tasty pieces. Ideally, make this in a wok with home made vegetable stock.

SERVES 4
2 tbsp groundnut or sunflower oil
7 oz smoked or marinated tofu, cubed
3 scallions, sliced diagonally
2 garlic cloves, cut in thin strips
1 carrot, thinly sliced in rounds
5 cups stock
2 tbsp soy sauce
1 tbsp dry sherry or vermouth
1 tsp sugar
4 oz Oak leaf or Romaine lettuce,
  shredded
salt and ground black pepper

1 Heat the oil in a wok, then stir-fry the tofu cubes until browned. Drain and set aside on kitchen paper.

2 In the same oil, stir-fry the scallions, garlic and carrot for 2 minutes. Pour in the stock, soy sauce, sherry or vermouth and sugar.

3 Bring to a boil and cook for 1 minute or so. Stir in the lettuce until it just wilts. Add the tofu, season to taste and serve the soup immediately.

Spiced Indian Cauliflower Soup

Light and tasty, this creamy, mildly spicy soup is multi-purpose. It makes a wonderful warming first course, an appetizing quick meal and – when served chilled – is delicious for any summer menu.

SERVES 4–6
1 large potato, peeled and diced
1 small cauliflower, chopped
1 onion, chopped
1 tbsp sunflower oil
1 garlic clove, crushed
1 tbsp fresh ginger, grated
2 tsp ground turmeric
1 tsp cumin seeds
1 tsp black mustard seeds
2 tsp ground coriander
4 cups vegetable stock
1¼ cups natural yogurt
salt and ground black pepper
fresh coriander or parsley, to garnish

1 Put the potato, cauliflower and onion into a large saucepan with the oil and 3 tbsp water. Heat until hot and bubbling, then cover and turn the heat down. Continue cooking the mixture for about 10 minutes.

2 Add the garlic, ginger and spices. Stir well and cook for another 2 minutes, stirring occasionally. Pour in the stock and season well. Bring to a boil, then cover and simmer for about 20 minutes. Stir in the yogurt, season well and garnish with coriander or parsley.

Winter Warmer Soup

Simmer a selection of popular winter root vegetables together for a warming and satisfying soup. Its creamy taste comes from adding cream or yogurt just before serving.

SERVES 6
3 medium carrots, chopped
1 large potato, chopped
1 large parsnip, chopped
1 large turnip or small rutabaga, chopped
1 onion, chopped
2 tbsp sunflower oil
2 tbsp butter
6 cups water
salt and ground black pepper
1 piece fresh ginger root, peeled and grated
1¼ cups milk
3 tbsp heavy cream, sour cream or natural yogurt
2 tbsp fresh dill, chopped

1 Put the carrots, potato, parsnip, turnip or rutabaga and onion into a large saucepan with the oil and butter. Fry lightly, then cover and sweat the vegetables on a very low heat for 15 minutes, shaking the pan occasionally.

2 Pour in the water, bring to a boil and season well. Cover and simmer for 20 minutes until the vegetables are soft.

3 Strain the vegetables, reserving the stock, add the ginger and purée in a food processor or blender until smooth.

4 Return the purée and stock to the pan. Add the milk and stir while the soup gently reheats.

5 Remove from the heat, stir in the heavy cream, sour cream or yogurt plus the dill, lemon juice and extra seasoning, if necessary. Reheat the soup, if you wish, but do not allow it to boil as you do so, or it may curdle.

Cream of Mushroom Soup

Home made mushroom soup is quite different from canned or packaged soups. Add a few shiitake mushrooms (which are more readily available) to give your soup a richer flavor.

SERVES 4–6
1 lb white mushrooms, sliced
4 oz shiitake mushrooms, sliced
3 tbsp sunflower oil
1 onion, chopped
1 stalk celery, chopped
5 cups stock or water
2 tbsp soy sauce
¼ cup long grain rice
salt and ground black pepper
1¼ cups milk
fresh parsley, chopped, or almond flakes, to garnish

1 Put all the mushrooms into a large saucepan with the oil, onion and celery. Heat until sizzling, then cover and simmer for about 10 minutes, shaking the pan occasionally.

2 Add the stock or water, soy sauce, rice and seasoning. Bring to a boil then cover and simmer gently for 20 minutes until the vegetables and rice are soft.

3 Strain the vegetables, reserving the stock, and purée until smooth in a food processor or blender. Return the vegetables and reserved stock to the pan.

4 Stir in the milk, reheat until boiling and taste for seasoning. Serve hot sprinkled with a little chopped parsley and a few almond flakes.

Classic Minestrone

This famous Italian soup has been much imitated around the world – with varying results. The home made version is a delicious revelation and also extremely healthy with pasta, beans and fresh vegetables.

SERVES 4
1 large leek, thinly sliced
2 carrots, chopped
1 zucchini, thinly sliced
4 oz whole green beans, halved
2 stalks celery, thinly sliced
3 tbsp olive oil
6¼ cups stock or water
1 × 14 oz can chopped tomatoes
1 tbsp fresh basil, chopped
1 tsp fresh thyme leaves, chopped
  or ½ tsp dried thyme
salt and ground black pepper
1 × 14 oz can cannellini or kidney beans
⅓ cup small pasta shapes such as tubetti
  or macaroni
fresh Parmesan cheese, finely grated, to
  garnish (optional)
fresh parsley, chopped, to garnish

1 Put all the fresh vegetables into a large saucepan with the olive oil. Heat until sizzling then cover, lower the heat and sweat the vegetables for 15 minutes, shaking the pan occasionally.

2 Add the stock or water, tomatoes, herbs and seasoning. Bring to the boil, replace the lid and simmer gently for about 30 minutes.

3 Add the beans and their liquor together with the pasta, and simmer for a further 10 minutes. Check the seasoning and serve hot sprinkled with the Parmesan cheese (if used) and parsley.

COOK'S TIP

Minestrone is also delicious served cold on a hot summer's day. In fact the flavor improves if made a day or two ahead and stored in the refrigerator. It can also be frozen and reheated.

Mediterranean Vegetables with Tahini

Wonderfully colorful, this starter is easily prepared in advance. For an *al fresco* meal, why not grill the vegetables on a barbecue? Tahini is a paste made from sesame seeds.

SERVES 4

2 peppers, red, green or yellow, seeded and quartered
2 zucchini, halved lengthways
2 small eggplants, seeded and halved lengthwise
1 fennel bulb, quartered
olive oil
salt and ground black pepper
4 oz Greek Halloumi cheese, sliced

TAHINI CREAM

1 cup tahini paste
1 garlic cloves, crushed
2 tbsp olive oil
2 tbsp fresh lemon juice
½ cup cold water

1 Preheat the broiler or barbecue until hot. Brush the vegetables with the oil and broil until just browned, turning once. (If the peppers begin to blacken, don't worry. The skins can be peeled off.) Cook the vegetables until just softened.

2 Place the vegetables in a shallow dish and season. Allow to cool. Meanwhile, brush the cheese slices with oil and grill these on both sides until just charred. Remove them with a spatula.

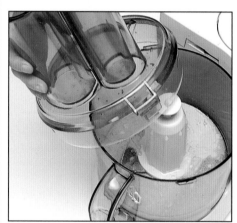

3 To make the tahini cream, place all the ingredients, except the water, in a food processor or blender. Whizz for a few seconds to mix, then, with the motor still running, pour in the water and blend until smooth.

4 Serve the vegetables and cheese on a platter and trickle over the cream. Delicious served with warm pitta or naan breads.

Imam Bayildi

Legend has it that a Muslim holy man – the Imam – was so overwhelmed by this dish that he fainted in sheer delight! Translated, Imam Bayildi means "The Imam fainted."

SERVES 4
2 medium eggplants, seeded (see Cook's Tip) and halved lengthwise
salt
4 tbsp olive oil
2 large onions, sliced thinly
2 garlic cloves, crushed
1 green pepper, seeded and sliced
1 × 14 oz can chopped tomatoes
1½ oz sugar
1 tsp ground coriander
ground black pepper
2 tbsp fresh coriander or parsley, chopped

1 Using a sharp knife, slash the flesh of the eggplants a few times. Sprinkle with salt and place in a colander for about half an hour. Rinse well and pat dry.

2 Gently fry the eggplants, cut side down, in the oil for 5 minutes, then drain and place in a shallow ovenproof dish.

3 In the same pan gently fry the onions, garlic and green pepper, adding extra oil if necessary. Cook for about 10 minutes, until the vegetables have softened.

4 Add the tomatoes, sugar, ground coriander and seasoning and cook for about 5 minutes until the mixture is reduced. Stir in the chopped coriander or parsley.

5 Spoon this mixture on top of the eggplants. Preheat the oven to 375°F, cover and bake for about 30–35 minutes. When cooked, cool, then chill. Serve cold with crusty bread.

COOK'S TIP

To prepare eggplants: sprinkle cut slices with salt and allow the juices that form to drain away in a colander. After 30 minutes or so, rinse well and pat dry. Eggplants prepared like this are less bitter and easier to cook.

Tricolor Salad

This can be a simple starter if served on individual salad plates, or part of a light buffet meal laid out on a platter. When lightly salted, tomatoes make their own flavorsome dressing with their natural juices.

SERVES 4–6
1 small red onion, sliced thinly
6 large full-flavored tomatoes
extra virgin olive oil, to sprinkle
2 oz/small bunch rocket or watercress,
   roughly chopped
salt and ground black pepper
6 oz Mozzarella cheese, thinly sliced or
   grated
2 tbsp pine nuts (optional)

1 Soak the onion slices in a bowl of cold water for 30 minutes, then drain and pat dry. Skin the tomatoes by slashing and dipping briefly in boiling water. Remove the core and slice the flesh.

2 Slice the tomatoes and arrange half on a large platter, or divide them between small plates.

3 Sprinkle liberally with olive oil, then layer with the chopped rocket or cress and soaked onion slices, seasoning well. Add in the cheese, sprinkling over more oil and seasoning as you go.

4 Repeat with the remaining tomato slices, salad leaves, cheese and oil.

5 Season well to finish and complete with some oil and a good scattering of pine nuts. Cover the salad and chill for at least 2 hours before serving.

Guacamole Salsa in Red Leaves

This lovely, light summery starter looks so attractive arranged in cups of radicchio leaves. Serve with chunks of warm garlic bread.

SERVES 4
2 tomatoes, skinned and chopped
1 tbsp grated onion
1 garlic clove, crushed
1 green chili, halved, seeded and
   chopped
2 ripe avocadoes
2 tbsp olive oil
½ tsp ground cumin
2 tbsp fresh coriander or parsley, chopped
juice of 1 lime
salt and ground black pepper
leaves from radicchio lettuce

1 Using a sharp knife, slash a small cross on the top of the tomatoes, then dip them briefly in a bowl of boiling water. The skins will slip off easily. Remove the core and chop the flesh.

2 Put the tomato flesh into a bowl together with the onion, garlic and chopped chili. Halve and pit the avocadoes, then scoop the flesh into the bowl, mashing it with a fork.

3 Add the remaining ingredients, except for the radicchio leaves, and mix well together, seasoning to taste.

4 Lay the radicchio leaves on a platter and spoon in the salsa. Serve immediately as avocadoes go black when exposed to the air.

COOK'S TIP

Take care when cutting chilies. The juice can sting, so be careful not to rub your eyes until you have washed your hands.

Tempura Vegetables with Dipping Sauce

A Japanese favorite, these are thinly sliced, fresh vegetables fried in a light crispy batter and served with a small bowl of flavored soy sauce. For the best results, serve these immediately so the batter remains crisp. Tempura also makes a delicious party piece.

SERVES 4–6
1 medium zucchini, sliced in thin sticks
1 red pepper, seeded and cut in wedges
3 large mushrooms, quartered
1 fennel bulb, cut in wedges with root attached
½ medium eggplant, thinly sliced
oil, for deep frying
SAUCE
3 tbsp soy sauce
1 tbsp medium dry sherry
1 tsp sesame seed oil
few shreds fresh ginger or scallion
BATTER
1 egg
1 cup all-purpose flour
¾ cup cold water
salt and ground black pepper

1 Prepare all the vegetables and lay them out on a tray, together with sheets of paper towel for draining the vegetables after cooking.

2 Mix the sauce ingredients together by whisking them in a bowl or shaking them together in a sealed jar. Pour into a bowl.

3 Half fill a deep frying pan with oil and preheat to a temperature of about 375°F. Quickly whisk the batter ingredients together but don't overbeat them. It doesn't matter if the batter is a little lumpy.

4 Fry the vegetables in stages by dipping a few quickly into the batter and lowering into the hot oil in a wire basket. Fry for just a minute until golden brown and crisp. Drain on the paper towel.

5 Repeat until all the vegetables are fried. Keep those you have cooked, uncovered, in a warm oven while you fry the rest. Serve the vegetables on a large platter alongside the dipping sauce.

COOK'S TIP

Successful deep frying can be quite tricky and a bit hazardous. First, be sure never to leave the pan of oil unattended while the heat is turned on. If you have to leave the stove, then turn the oil off. The oil will drop in temperature during cooking so keep re-heating it between batches.

Corn Blinis with Dill Cream

A mouth-watering and unusual starter, these blinis are also suitable for a cocktail buffet. Ideally make them an hour or two before you serve them, although the batter will stand for longer.

SERVES 6–8
¾ cup all-purpose flour
⅔ cup whole wheat flour
1 cup buttermilk
4 small eggs, beaten
½ tsp salt
½ tsp baking powder
2 tbsp butter, melted
good pinch baking soda
1 tbsp hot water
1 × 7 oz can corn kernels, drained
oil, for the griddle
DILL CREAM
7 oz sour cream
2 tbsp fresh dill, chopped
2 tbsp fresh chives, chopped
salt and ground black pepper

1 Mix the two flours and buttermilk together until completely smooth. Cover and leave to chill for about 8 hours in the refrigerator.

2 Beat in the eggs, salt, baking powder and butter. Mix the baking soda with the hot water and add this too, along with the corn kernels.

3 Heat a griddle or heavy based frying pan until quite hot. Brush with a little oil and drop spoonfuls of the blinis mixture on to it. The mixture should start to sizzle immediately.

4 Cook until holes appear on the top and the mixture looks almost set. Using a spatula, flip the blinis over and cook briefly. Stack the blinis under a clean dish towel while you make the rest.

5 To make the cream, simply blend the sour cream with the herbs and seasoning. Serve the blinis with a few spoonfuls of cream and garnished with sliced radishes and herbs.

LIGHT LUNCHES & SUPPERS

For tempting lunches that are not too filling and tasty television suppers,
experiment with these glorious recipes, from those that include protein-rich
ingredients such as tofu to irresistible cheese and pasta dishes.

Mushroom and Chili Carbonara

For a richer mushroom flavor, use a small package of dried Italian porcini mushrooms in this quick egg sauce, and for an extra spicy zing, toss in some chili flakes too.

SERVES 4
1 × ½ oz package dried porcini
  mushrooms
1¼ cups hot water
8 oz spaghetti
1 garlic clove, crushed
2 tbsp butter
1 tbsp olive oil
8 oz button or field mushrooms, sliced
1 tsp dried chili flakes
2 eggs
1¼ cups light cream
salt and ground black pepper
fresh Parmesan cheese, grated, and
  parsley, chopped, to serve

1 Soak the dried mushrooms in the hot water for 15 minutes, drain and reserve the liquor.

2 Boil the spaghetti according to the instructions on the package in salted water. Drain and rinse in cold water.

3 In a large saucepan, lightly sauté the garlic with the butter and oil for half a minute then add the mushrooms, including the soaked porcini ones, and the dried chili flakes, and stir well. Cook for about 2 minutes, stirring a few times.

4 Pour in the reserved mushroom stock and boil to reduce slightly.

5 Beat the eggs with the cream and season well. Return the cooked spaghetti to the pan and toss in the eggs and cream. Reheat, without boiling, and serve hot sprinkled with Parmesan cheese and chopped parsley.

VARIATION

Instead of mushrooms, try using either finely sliced and sautéed leeks or perhaps coarsely shredded lettuce with peas. If chili flakes are too hot and spicy for you, then try the delicious alternative of skinned and chopped tomatoes with torn, fresh basil leaves.

Tagliatelle with Hit-the-pan Salsa

It is possible to make a hot filling meal within just fifteen minutes with this quick-cook salsa sauce. If you don't have time to peel the tomatoes, then don't bother.

SERVES 2
8 oz tagliatelle
3 tbsp olive oil, preferably extra virgin
3 large tomatoes
1 garlic clove, crushed
4 scallions, sliced
1 green chili, halved, seeded and sliced
juice of 1 orange (optional)
2 tbsp fresh parsley, chopped
salt and ground black pepper
cheese, grated, to garnish (optional)

1 Boil the tagliatelle in plenty of salted water until it is *al dente*. Drain and toss in a little of the oil. Season well.

2 Skin the tomatoes by dipping them briefly in a bowl of boiling water. The skins should slip off easily. Chop the tomatoes roughly.

3 Heat the remaining oil until it is quite hot and stir-fry the garlic, onions and chili for a minute. The pan should sizzle.

4 Add the tomatoes, orange juice (if using) and parsley. Season well and stir in the tagliatelle to reheat. Serve with the grated cheese (if used).

COOK'S TIP

You could use any pasta shape for this recipe. It would be particularly good with large rigatoni or linguini, or as a sauce for fresh ravioli or tortellini.

Potato and Cabbage Croquettes

This London breakfast dish is enjoying something of a revival. Originally made on Mondays with leftover potatoes and cabbage from the Sunday lunch, it is suitable for any light meal occasion. For breakfast, serve the croquettes with eggs, grilled tomatoes and mushrooms.

SERVES 4
1 lb/3 cups mashed potato
8 oz steamed or boiled cabbage or kale, shredded
1 egg, beaten
4 oz Cheddar cheese, grated
fresh nutmeg, grated
salt and ground black pepper
all-purpose flour, for coating
oil, for frying

1 Mix the potatoes with the cabbage or kale, egg, cheese, nutmeg and seasoning. Divide and shape into eight croquettes.

2 Chill for an hour or so, if possible, as this enables the mixture to become firm and makes it easier to fry. Toss the croquettes in the flour. Heat about ½ in of oil in a frying pan until it is quite hot.

3 Carefully slide the croquettes into the oil and fry on each side for about 3 minutes until golden and crisp. Drain on paper towel and serve hot and crisp.

Cheese and Chutney Toasts

Quick cheese on toast can be made quite memorable with a few tasty additions. Serve these scrumptious toasties with a simple salad.

SERVES 4
4 slices whole wheat bread, thickly sliced
butter or margarine
4 oz Cheddar cheese, grated
1 tsp dried thyme
ground black pepper
2 tbsp chutney or relish

1 Preheat the broiler. Toast the bread slices lightly on each side, then spread sparingly with butter or margarine.

2 Mix the cheese and thyme together and season with pepper.

3 Spread the chutney or relish on the toast and divide the cheese between the four slices.

4 Return to the broiler and cook until browned and bubbling. Cut into halves, diagonally, and serve with salad.

Risotto Primavera

Real Italian risottos should be creamy and full of flavor. They are best made freshly and do need frequent stirring, but this can be done in between other jobs in the kitchen. For best results use a quality Arborio rice which has a good *al dente* bite.

SERVES 4

4 cups hot vegetable stock, preferably home made
1 red onion, chopped
2 garlic cloves, crushed
2 tbsp olive oil
2 tbsp butter
1¼ cups risotto rice (do not rinse)
3 tbsp dry white wine
4 oz asparagus spears or green beans, sliced and blanched
2 young carrots, sliced and blanched
2 oz baby button mushrooms
salt and ground black pepper
2 oz Pecorino or Parmesan cheese, grated

1 It is important to follow the steps for making real risotto so that you achieve the right texture. First, heat the stock in a saucepan to simmering.

2 Next to it, in a large saucepan, sauté the onion and garlic in the oil and butter for 3 minutes.

3 Stir in the rice, making sure each grain is coated well in the oil, then stir in the wine. Allow to reduce down and spoon in two ladles of hot stock, stirring continuously.

4 Allow this to bubble down, then add more stock and stir again. Continue like this, ladling in the stock and stirring frequently for up to 20 minutes, by which time the rice will have swelled greatly.

5 Mix in the asparagus or beans, carrots and mushrooms, seasoning well, and cook for a minute or two more. Serve immediately in bowls with a scattering of grated cheese.

VARIATION

If you have any leftover risotto, shape it into small balls and then coat in beaten egg and dried bread crumbs. Chill for 30 minutes before deep frying in hot oil until golden and crisp.

Kitchiri

This is the Indian original which inspired the classic breakfast dish known as kedgeree. Made with basmati rice and small tasty lentils this will make an ample supper or brunch dish.

SERVES 4

1 cup Indian masoor dhal or green lentils
1 garlic clove, crushed
4 tbsp vegetarian ghee or butter
2 tbsp sunflower oil
1¼ cups easy-cook basmati rice
2 tsp ground coriander
2 tsp cumin seeds
2 cloves
3 cardamom pods
2 bay leaves
1 stick cinnamon
4 cups stock
2 tbsp tomato paste
salt and ground black pepper
3 tbsp fresh coriander or parsley, chopped

1 Cover the dhal or lentils with boiling water and soak for 30 minutes. Drain and boil in fresh water for 10 minutes. Drain once more and set aside.

2 Fry the onion and garlic in the ghee or butter and oil in a large saucepan for about 5 minutes.

3 Add the rice, stir well to coat the grains in the ghee or butter and oil, then stir in the spices. Cook gently for a minute or so.

4 Add the lentils, stock, tomato paste and seasoning. Bring to a boil, then cover and simmer for 20 minutes until the stock is absorbed and the lentils and rice are just soft. Stir in the coriander or parsley and check the seasoning. Remove the cinnamon stick and bay leaf.

Baked Potatoes and Three Fillings

Potatoes baked in their skins and packed with a variety of fillings make an excellent and nourishing meal. Although they have been cooked here in a conventional oven, potatoes can be baked more quickly and just as successfully in a microwave.

4 medium size baking potatoes
olive oil, for greasing
sea salt, to serve

1 Preheat the oven to 400°F. Score the potatoes with a cross and rub all over with the olive oil.

2 Place on a baking sheet and cook for 45–60 minutes until a knife inserted into the centers indicates they are cooked.

3 Cut the potatoes open along the score lines and push up the flesh from the base with your fingers. Season with salt and fill with your chosen filling.

EACH FILLING IS FOR FOUR POTATOES

RED BEAN FILLING
1 × 15 oz can red kidney beans
7 oz low fat cottage or cream cheese
2 tbsp mild chili sauce
1 tsp ground cumin

Red Bean – drain the beans, heat in a pan or microwave and stir in the cream cheese, chili sauce and cumin.

SOY VEGETABLES FILLING
2 leeks, thinly sliced
2 carrots, cut in sticks
1 zucchini, thinly sliced
4 oz baby corn, halved
3 tbsp groundnut or sunflower oil
4 oz button mushrooms, sliced
3 tbsp soy sauce
2 tbsp dry sherry or vermouth
1 tbsp sesame oil
sesame seeds, to sprinkle

Soy Vegetables – stir-fry the leeks, carrots, zucchini and baby corn in the oil for about 2 minutes, then add the mushrooms and cook for a further minute. Mix together the soy sauce, sherry and sesame oil and pour over the vegetables. Heat through until just bubbling and then scatter over the sesame seeds.

CHEESE AND CREAMED CORN FILLING
1 × 15 oz can creamed corn
4 oz cheese, grated
1 tsp dried mixed herbs

Cheese and creamed corn – heat the corn, add the cheese and mixed herbs.

Peanut Butter Fingers

Children will love these crispy, tasty croquettes. Make up a batch and freeze some ready for whenever there are young tummies to fill!

MAKES 12
2 lb potatoes
1 large onion, chopped
2 large peppers, red or green, chopped
3 carrots, coarsely grated
3 tbsp sunflower oil
2 zucchini, coarsely grated
4 oz mushrooms, chopped
1 tbsp dried mixed herbs
4 oz sharp Cheddar cheese, grated
½ cup crunchy peanut butter
salt and ground black pepper
2 eggs, beaten
about ½ cup dried breadcrumbs
3 tbsp grated Parmesan cheese
oil, for deep frying

1 Boil the potatoes until tender, then drain well and mash. Set aside.

2 Fry the onion, peppers and carrots gently in the oil for about 5 minutes then add the zucchini and mushrooms. Cook for 5 minutes more.

3 Mix the potato with the dried mixed herbs, grated cheese and peanut butter. Season, allow to cool for 30 minutes, then stir in one of the eggs.

4 Spread out on a large plate, cool and chill, then divide into 12 portions and shape. Dip your hands in cold water if the mixture sticks.

5 Put the second egg in a bowl and dip the potato fingers into it first, then into the crumbs and Parmesan cheese until coated evenly. Return to the fridge to set.

6 Heat the oil in a deep fat frier to 375°F then fry the fingers in batches for about 3 minutes until golden. Drain well on paper towel. Serve hot.

COOK'S TIP

To reheat, thaw for 1 hour, then oven bake at 375°F for 15 minutes.

Pasta Salade Tiède

Boil a pan of pasta shapes and toss with vinaigrette dressing and some freshly prepared salad vegetables, and you have the basis for a delicious warm salad.

SERVES 2
4 oz pasta shapes, e.g. shells
3 tbsp vinaigrette dressing
3 sun-dried tomatoes in oil, snipped
2 scallions, sliced
2 or 3 sprigs watercress or arugula, chopped
¼ cucumber, halved, seeded and sliced
salt and ground black pepper
about 1½ oz Pecorino cheese, coarsely grated

1 Boil the pasta according to the instructions on the package. Drain and toss in the dressing.

2 Mix in the tomatoes, onions, cress or arugula and cucumber. Season to taste.

3 Divide between two plates and sprinkle over the cheese. Eat at room temperature, if possible.

Penne with "Can Can" Sauce

The quality of canned beans and tomatoes is so good that it is possible to transform them into a very fresh tasting pasta sauce in minutes. Again, choose whatever pasta you like.

SERVES 3—4
8 oz penne pasta
1 onion, sliced
1 red pepper, seeded and sliced
2 tbsp olive oil
1 × 14 oz can chopped tomatoes
1 × 15 oz can chick peas
2 tbsp dry vermouth (optional)
1 tsp dried oregano
1 large bay leaf
2 tbsp capers
salt and ground black pepper

1 Boil the pasta as instructed on the package, then drain. In a saucepan, gently fry the onion and pepper in the oil for about 5 minutes, stirring occasionally, until softened.

2 Add the tomatoes, chick peas with their liquor, vermouth (if liked), herbs and capers.

3 Season and bring to a boil then simmer for about 10 minutes. Remove the bay leaf and mix in the pasta, reheat and serve hot.

Tofu and Crunchy Vegetables

High protein, wonder food tofu is nicest if marinated lightly before cooking. If you use the smoked tofu, it's even tastier. For successful stir-frying, make sure all your ingredients are prepared first.

SERVES 4
2 × 8 oz cartons smoked tofu, cubed
3 tbsp soy sauce
2 tbsp dry sherry or vermouth
1 tbsp sesame oil
3 tbsp groundnut or sunflower oil
2 leeks, thinly sliced
2 carrots, cut in sticks
1 large zucchini, thinly sliced
4 oz baby corn, halved
4 oz button or shiitake mushrooms, sliced
1 tbsp sesame seeds
1 package of egg noodles, cooked

1 Marinate the tofu in the soy sauce, sherry or vermouth and sesame oil for at least half an hour. Drain and reserve the marinade.

2 Heat the groundnut or sunflower oil in a wok and stir-fry the tofu cubes until browned all over. Remove and reserve.

3 Stir-fry the leeks, carrots, zucchini and baby corn, stirring and tossing for about 2 minutes. Add the mushrooms and cook for a further minute.

4 Return the tofu to the wok and pour in the marinade. Heat until bubbling, then scatter over the sesame seeds.

5 Serve as soon as possible with the hot cooked noodles, dressed in a little sesame oil, if liked.

VARIATION

Tofu is also excellent marinated and skewered, then lightly grilled. Push the tofu off the skewers into pockets of pitta bread. Fill with lemon-dressed salad and serve with a final trickle of tahini cream.

Egg Foo Yung

A great way of turning a bowl of leftover cooked rice into a meal for four, this Oriental dish is tasty and full of texture. Use bought bean sprouts or grow your own – it's easy and fun.

SERVES 4
salt and ground black pepper
3 eggs, beaten
good pinch five spice powder (optional)
3 tbsp groundnut or sunflower oil
4 scallions, sliced
1 garlic clove, crushed
1 small green pepper, seeded and
  chopped
4 oz fresh bean sprouts
3 cups cooked white rice
3 tbsp light soy sauce
1 tbsp sesame oil

1 Season the eggs and beat in the five spice powder, if using.

2 In a wok or large frying pan, heat one tablespoon of the oil and when quite hot, pour in the egg.

3 Cook rather like an omelet, pulling the mixture away from the sides and allowing the rest to slip underneath.

4 Cook the egg until firm then tip out. Chop the "omelet" into small strips.

5 Heat the remaining oil and stir-fry the scallions, garlic, pepper and bean sprouts for about 2 minutes, stirring and tossing continuously.

6 Mix in the rice and heat thoroughly, stirring well. Add the soy sauce and sesame oil then return the egg and mix in well. Serve immediately, piping hot.

Light Ratatouille

This lightly cooked medley of fresh vegetables is cooked with simple poached eggs and served topped with crisply fried bread crumbs.

SERVES 4
3 tbsp olive oil
1 cup fresh white bread crumbs
1 yellow or red pepper, seeded and thinly sliced
2 garlic cloves, crushed
2 leeks, thinly sliced
2 zucchini, thinly sliced
2 tomatoes, skinned and sliced
1 tsp dried rosemary, crushed
4 eggs
salt and ground black pepper

1 Heat half the oil in a shallow fireproof dish (or frying pan with a lid) and fry the bread crumbs until they are golden and crisp. Drain on paper towel.

2 Add the remaining oil and fry the pepper, garlic and leeks in the same pan for about 10 minutes until softened.

3 Add the zucchini, tomatoes and rosemary and cook for a further 5 minutes. Season well.

4 Using the back of a spoon, make four wells in the vegetable mixture and break an egg into each one. Lightly season the eggs then cover and cook on a gentle heat for about 3 minutes until they are just set.

5 Sprinkle over the crisp bread crumbs and serve immediately, piping hot.

Macaroni Soufflé

This is generally a great favorite with children, and is rather like a light and fluffy macaroni and cheese. Make sure you serve a soufflé the moment it is cooked or it will sink dramatically.

SERVES 3–4
6 oz short cut macaroni
melted butter, to coat
6 tbsp dried bread crumbs
8 tbsp butter
2 tsp ground paprika
⅔ cup all-purpose flour
2½ cups milk
6 oz Cheddar or Gruyère cheese, grated
4 oz Parmesan cheese, grated
salt and ground black pepper
6 eggs, separated

1 Preheat the oven to 300°F. Boil the macaroni according to the package instructions. Drain and set aside.

2 Brush the insides of a 1 quart soufflé dish with melted butter and then coat evenly with the bread crumbs, shaking out any excess.

3 Put the butter, paprika, flour and milk into a saucepan and bring to a boil slowly, whisking it constantly until it is smooth and thick.

4 Simmer the sauce for a minute, then take off the heat and stir in the cheeses until they melt. Season well and mix with the macaroni.

5 Beat in the egg yolks. Whisk the egg whites until they form soft peaks and spoon a quarter into the sauce mixture, beating it gently to loosen it up.

6 Using a large metal spoon, carefully fold in the rest of the egg whites and transfer to the prepared soufflé dish.

7 Bake in the center of the oven for about 40–45 minutes until the soufflé has risen and is golden brown. The middle should wobble very slightly and the soufflé should be lightly creamy inside.

Cowboy Hot Pot

A great dish to serve as a children's main meal, which adults will enjoy too – if they are allowed to join the posse. You can use any vegetable mixture you like, although beans are a must for every self-respecting cowboy!

SERVES 4–6
1 onion, sliced
1 red pepper, sliced
1 sweet potato or 2 carrots, chopped
3 tbsp sunflower oil
4 oz green beans, chopped
1 × 14 oz can baked beans
1 × 7 oz can corn
1 tbsp tomato paste
1 tsp barbecue spice seasoning
4 oz Gouda or Edam cheese (preferably smoked), cubed
1 lb potatoes, thinly sliced
2 tbsp butter, melted
salt and ground black pepper

1 Fry the onion, pepper and sweet potato or carrots gently in the oil until softened but not browned.

2 Add the green beans, baked beans, corn (and liquor), tomato paste and barbecue spice seasoning. Bring to a boil, then simmer for 5 minutes.

3 Transfer the vegetables to a shallow ovenproof dish and then scatter with the cubed cheese.

4 Cover the vegetable and cheese mixture with the sliced potato, brush with butter, season and then bake at 375°F for 30–40 minutes until golden brown on top and the potato is cooked.

Stir-fried Rice and Vegetables

If you have some left-over cooked rice and a few vegetables lurking at the bottom of the refrigerator, then you've got the basis for this quick and tasty meal.

SERVES 4
½ cucumber
2 scallions, sliced
1 garlic clove, crushed
2 carrots, thinly sliced
1 small red or yellow pepper, seeded and sliced
3 tbsp sunflower or groundnut oil
¼ small green cabbage, shredded
4 cups cooked long grain rice
2 tbsp light soy sauce
1 tbsp sesame oil
salt and ground black pepper
fresh parsley or coriander, chopped (optional)
4 oz unsalted cashew nuts, almonds or peanuts

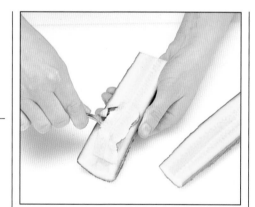

1 Halve the cucumber lengthwise and scoop out the seeds with a teaspoon. Slice the flesh diagonally. Set aside.

2 In a wok or large frying pan, stir-fry the scallions, garlic, carrots and pepper in the oil for about 3 minutes until they are just soft.

3 Add the cabbage and cucumber and fry for another minute or two until the leaves begin to just wilt. Mix in the rice, soy sauce, sesame oil and seasoning. Reheat the mixture thoroughly, stirring and tossing all the time.

4 Add the herbs, if using, and nuts. Check the seasoning and serve piping hot.

Pepper and Potato Tortilla

A great favorite with my family, tortilla is rather like a thick omelette or pastry-less quiche. Traditionally a Spanish dish, it is best eaten cold in chunky wedges. Tortilla makes ideal picnicking food. Use a hard Spanish cheese, like Mahon, or a goat cheese, if you can, although sharp Cheddar makes a good substitute.

SERVES 4
2 medium size potatoes
3 tbsp olive oil
1 large onion, thinly sliced
2 garlic cloves, crushed
2 peppers, one green and one red, thinly sliced
6 eggs, beaten
4 oz sharp cheese, grated
salt and ground black pepper

1 Do not peel the potatoes, but wash them thoroughly. Par boil them as they are for about 10 minutes, then drain and slice them thickly. Switch on the broiler so that it has time to warm up while you prepare the tortilla.

2 In a large non-stick or well seasoned frying pan, heat the oil and fry the onion, garlic and peppers on a moderate heat for 5 minutes until softened.

3 Add the potatoes and continue frying, stirring occasionally until the potatoes are completely cooked and the vegetables are soft. Add a little extra oil if the pan seems rather dry.

4 Pour in half the eggs, then sprinkle over half the cheese then the rest of the egg, seasoning as you go. Finish with a layer of cheese.

5 Continue to cook on a low heat, without stirring, half covering the pan with a lid to help set the eggs.

6 When the mixture is firm, flash the pan under the hot broiler to seal the top just lightly. Leave the tortilla in the pan to cool. This helps it firm up further and makes it easier to turn out.

VARIATION

You can add any sliced and lightly cooked vegetable, such as mushrooms, zucchini or broccoli, to this tortilla dish instead of the green and red peppers. Cooked pasta or brown rice are both excellent alternatives too.

Cauliflower and Egg Casserole

No need to make a traditional bechamel sauce for this country classic. A quick all-in-one sauce can be made in minutes while a small package of soup croûtons gives the dish a delicious crunchy topping.

SERVES 4
1 medium size cauliflower, broken in
   florets
1 medium onion, sliced
2 eggs, hard boiled, peeled and chopped
3 tbsp whole wheat flour
1 tsp mild curry powder
2 tbsp sunflower margarine or other low
   fat spread
2 cups milk
½ tsp dried thyme
salt and ground black pepper
4 oz sharp cheese, grated
small package of soup croûtons

1 Boil the cauliflower and onion in enough salted water to cover until they are just tender. Be careful not to overcook them. Drain well.

2 Arrange the cauliflower and onion in a shallow ovenproof dish and scatter over the chopped egg.

3 Put the flour, curry powder, fat and milk in a saucepan all together. Bring slowly to a boil, stirring well until thickened and smooth. Stir in the thyme and seasoning and allow the sauce to simmer for a minute or two. Remove the pan from the heat and stir in about three quarters of the cheese.

4 Pour the sauce over the cauliflower, scatter over the croûtons and sprinkle with the remaining cheese. Brown under a hot broiler until golden and serve. Delicious with thick crusty bread.

Quorn with Ginger, Chili and Leeks

Quorn is a newly-developed, versatile mycoprotein food which easily absorbs different flavors and retains a good firm texture. This makes it ideal for stir-frying. It is available in most supermarkets.

SERVES 4

8 oz Quorn cubes
3 tbsp soy sauce
2 tbsp dry sherry or vermouth
2 tsp honey
⅔ cup stock
2 tsp corn starch
3 tbsp sunflower or groundnut oil
3 leeks, thinly sliced
1 red chili, seeded and sliced
1 in piece fresh ginger root, peeled and shredded
salt and ground black pepper

1 Toss the Quorn in the soy sauce and sherry or vermouth until well coated and leave to marinate for about 30 minutes.

2 Strain the Quorn from the marinade and reserve the juices in a jug. Mix the marinade with the honey, stock and corn starch to make a paste.

3 Heat the oil in a wok or large frying pan and when hot, stir-fry the Quorn until it is crisp on the outside. Remove the Quorn and set aside.

4 Reheat the oil and stir-fry the leeks, chili and ginger for about 2 minutes until they are just soft. Season lightly.

5 Return the Quorn to the pan, together with the marinade, and stir well until the liquid is thick and glossy. Serve hot with rice or egg noodles.

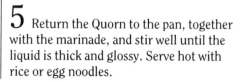

Chinese Potatoes with Chili Beans

East meets West. An American style dish with a Chinese flavor – the sauce is particularly tasty. Try it as a quick supper dish when you fancy a meal with a little zing!

SERVES 4
4 medium potatoes, cut in thick chunks
3 scallions, sliced
1 large fresh chili, seeded and sliced
2 tbsp sunflower or groundnut oil
2 garlic cloves, crushed
1 × 14 oz can red kidney beans, drained
2 tbsp soy sauce
1 tbsp sesame oil
TO SERVE
salt and ground black pepper
1 tbsp sesame seeds
fresh coriander or parsley, chopped, to garnish

1 Boil the potatoes until they are just tender. Take care not to overcook them. Drain and reserve.

2 In a large frying pan or wok, stir-fry the scallions and chili in the oil for about 1 minute, then add the garlic and fry for a few seconds longer.

3 Add the potatoes, stirring well, then the beans and finally the soy sauce and sesame oil.

4 Season to taste and cook the vegetables until they are well heated through. Sprinkle with the sesame seeds and the coriander or parsley.

Pitta Pizzas

Pitta breads make very good bases for quick thin and crispy pizzas, and they are easy to eat with your hands too. The perfect speedy snack.

SERVES 4

EXTRA TOPPINGS – CHOOSE FROM
1 small red onion, thinly sliced and lightly fried
mushrooms, sliced and fried
1 × 7 oz can corn, drained
jalapeno chilis, sliced
black or green olives, pitted and sliced
capers, drained

BASIC PIZZAS
4 pitta breads, ideally whole wheat
small jar of pasta sauce
8 oz Mozzarella cheese, sliced or grated
dried oregano or thyme, to sprinkle
salt and ground black pepper

1 Prepare two or three toppings of your choice for the pizzas.

2 Preheat the broiler and lightly toast the pitta breads on each side.

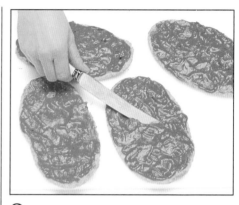

3 Spread pasta sauce on each pitta, right to the edge. This prevents the edges of the pitta from burning.

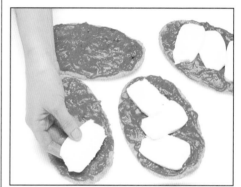

4 Arrange cheese slices or grated cheese on top of each pitta and sprinkle with herbs and seasoning.

5 Add the toppings of your choice and then broil the pizzas for about 5–8 minutes until they are golden brown and bubbling. Serve immediately.

Tagliatelle with Spinach and Soy Garlic Cheese

It's wonderful to mix ingredients from different cuisines and produce a delicious dish as a result. Italian pasta and spinach combine with Chinese soy and French garlic cream cheese to create this wonderful rich and mouth-watering dish.

SERVES 4
8 oz tagliatelle, preferably mixed colors
8 oz fresh leaf spinach, well washed
2 tbsp light soy sauce
3 oz carton garlic and herb cheese
3 tbsp milk
salt and ground black pepper

1 Boil the tagliatelle according to the instructions on the package and drain. Return the pasta to the pan.

2 Meanwhile blanch the spinach in a tiny amount of water until just wilted, then drain very well, squeezing dry with the back of a wooden spoon. Chop roughly with kitchen scissors.

3 Return the spinach to its pan and stir in the soy sauce, garlic and herb cheese and milk. Bring slowly to a boil, stirring until smooth. Season to taste.

4 When the sauce is ready, pour it over the pasta. Toss the pasta and sauce together well and serve hot.

Aduki Bean Burgers

Although not quick to make, these burgers are a delicious alternative to store-bought ones; so it is worth making up several batches for the freezer. Use a long-grain brown rice, not a quick cook variety.

MAKES 12
1 cup brown rice
1 onion, chopped
2 garlic cloves, crushed
2 tbsp sunflower oil
4 tbsp butter
1 small green pepper, seeded and
   chopped
1 carrot, coarsely grated
1 × 14 oz can aduki beans, drained (or
   4 oz dried weight, soaked and cooked)
1 egg, beaten
4 oz sharp cheese, grated
1 tsp dried thyme
½ cup roasted hazelnuts or toasted
   flaked almonds
salt and ground black pepper
whole wheat flour or cornmeal, for
   coating
oil, for deep frying

1 Cook the rice according to the instructions on the package, allowing it to slightly overcook so that it is softer. Strain the rice and transfer it to a large bowl.

2 Fry the onion and garlic in the oil and butter together with the green pepper and carrot for about 10 minutes until the vegetables are softened.

3 Mix this vegetable mixture into the rice, together with the aduki beans, egg, cheese, thyme, nuts or almonds and plenty of seasoning. Chill until quite firm.

4 Shape into 12 patties, using wet hands if the mixture sticks. Coat the patties in flour or cornmeal and set aside.

5 Heat ½ in oil in a large, shallow frying pan and fry the burgers in batches until browned on each side, about five minutes in total. Remove and drain on kitchen paper. Eat some burgers freshly cooked, and freeze the rest for later. Serve in buns with salad and relish.

COOK'S TIP

To freeze the burgers, cool them after cooking, then open freeze them before wrapping and bagging. Use within six weeks. Cook from frozen by baking in a pre-heated moderately hot oven for 20–25 minutes.

Zucchini Quiche

If possible, use a hard goat cheese for this quiche as its flavor complements the zucchini nicely. Bake the pastry shell first for a crisp crust.

SERVES 6
PASTRY
scant 1 cup whole wheat flour
1 cup all-purpose flour
½ cup sunflower margarine
FILLING
1 red onion, thinly sliced
2 tbsp olive oil
2 large zucchini, sliced
6 oz cheese, grated
2 tbsp fresh basil, chopped
3 eggs, beaten
1¼ cups milk
salt and ground black pepper

1 Preheat the oven to 400°F. Mix the flours together and rub in the margarine until it resembles crumbs, then mix to a firm dough with cold water.

2 Roll out the pastry and use it to line a 9–10 in pie pan, ideally at least 1 in deep. Prick the base, chill for 30 minutes then fill with waxed paper or foil and baking beans.

3 Bake the pastry shell on a baking sheet for 20 minutes, uncovering it for the last 5 minutes so that it can crisp up.

4 Meanwhile, sweat the onion in the oil for 5 minutes, until it is soft. Add the zucchini and fry for another 5 minutes.

5 Spoon the onions and zucchini into the pastry case. Scatter over most of the cheese and all of the basil.

6 Beat together the eggs, milk and seasoning and pour over the filling. Top with the remaining cheese.

7 Turn the oven down to 350°F and return the quiche for about 40 minutes until risen and just firm to the touch in the center. Allow to cool slightly before serving.

MAIN COURSES

Create healthy and satisfying meals that make the most of the wonderful variety of herbs and spices, as well as nutritious ingredients such as lentils, rice and vegetables.

Arabian Spinach

Stir-fry spinach with onions and spices; then mix in a can of chick peas and you have a delicious family main course meal in next to no time.

SERVES 4
1 onion, sliced
2 tbsp olive or sunflower oil
2 garlic cloves, crushed
14 oz spinach, washed and shredded
1 tsp cumin seeds
1 × 15 oz can chick peas, drained
knob of butter
salt and ground black pepper

1 In a large frying pan or wok, fry the onion in the oil for about 5 minutes until softened. Add the garlic and cumin seeds, then fry for another minute.

2 Add the spinach, in stages, stirring it until the leaves begin to wilt. Fresh spinach condenses down dramatically on cooking and it *will* all fit into the pan.

3 Stir in the chick peas, butter and seasoning. Reheat until just bubbling, then serve hot. Drain off any pan juices, if you like, but this dish is rather nice served slightly saucy.

Vegetable Medley with Lentil Bolognese

Instead of a white or cheese sauce, it makes a nice change to top a selection of lightly steamed vegetables with a healthy and delicious lentil sauce.

SERVES 6
1 small cauliflower, in florets
8 oz broccoli florets
2 leeks, thickly sliced
8 oz Brussels sprouts, halved if large
Lentil Bolognese sauce

1 Make up the sauce and keep warm.

2 Place all the vegetables in a steamer over a pan of boiling water and cook for 8–10 minutes until just tender.

3 Drain and place in a shallow serving dish. Spoon the sauce on top, stirring slightly to mix. Serve hot.

Falafel

Made with ground chick peas, herbs
and spices, falafel is a Middle Eastern
street food normally served tucked
into warm pitta breads with scoopfuls
of salad. It is absolutely delicious
served with tahini cream or dollops
of natural yogurt.

MAKES 8
1 × 15 oz can chick peas, drained
1 garlic clove, crushed
2 tbsp fresh parsley, chopped
2 tbsp fresh coriander, chopped
1 tbsp fresh mint, chopped
1 tsp cumin seeds
2 tbsp fresh breadcrumbs
1 tsp salt
ground black pepper
oil, for deep frying

1 Grind the chick peas in a food
processor until they are just smooth, then
mix them with all the other ingredients
until you have a thick, creamy paste. Add
pepper to taste.

2 Using wet hands, shape the chick
pea mixture into 8 balls and chill for
30 minutes so that they become firm.

3 Meanwhile, heat about ¼ in of oil
in a shallow frying pan and fry the balls
a few at a time. Cook each one for about
8 minutes, turning them all carefully
just once.

4 Drain each ball on paper towel and fry
the rest in batches, reheating the oil in
between. Serve tucked inside warm pitta
breads with sliced salad, tomatoes and
tahini cream or yogurt.

COOK'S TIP

Falafel can be made in batches
and frozen. Allow the balls to
cool, spread out on wire racks and
open freeze until solid. Tip into a
freezer-proof plastic container. To
reheat, bake in a moderate oven
for 10–15 minutes.

Caribbean Rice and Peas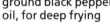

A great family favorite in West Indian
culture, this dish is not only very
tasty, but nutritionally well balanced
too. Serve with slices of fried
eggplant.

SERVES 4
1¼ cups quick cook unconverted long-
    grain rice
¾ cup dried gunga peas or red kidney
    beans, soaked and cooked but still firm
3⅔ cups water
2 oz creamed coconut, chopped
1 tsp dried thyme or 1 tbsp fresh thyme
    leaves
1 small onion stuck with 6 whole cloves
salt and ground black pepper

1 Put the rice and peas or kidney beans
into a large saucepan with the water,
coconut, thyme, onion and seasoning.

2 Bring to a boil, stirring until the
coconut melts. Cover and simmer gently
for 20 minutes.

3 Remove the lid and allow to cook
uncovered for 5 minutes to reduce down
any excess liquid. Remove from the heat
and stir occasionally to separate the
grains. The rice should be quite dry.

Greek Stuffed Vegetables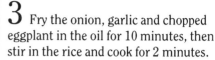

Vegetables such as peppers make wonderful containers for savory fillings. Instead of sticking to one type of vegetable, follow the Greeks' example and serve an interesting selection. Thick, creamy Greek yogurt is the ideal accompaniment.

SERVES 3–6
1 medium eggplant
1 large green pepper
2 large tomatoes
1 large onion, chopped
2 garlic cloves, crushed
3 tbsp olive oil
1 cup brown rice
2½ cups stock
¾ cup pine nuts
⅓ cup currants
salt and ground black pepper
3 tbsp fresh dill, chopped
3 tbsp fresh parsley, chopped
1 tbsp fresh mint, chopped
extra olive oil, to sprinkle
natural Greek yogurt, to serve
fresh sprigs of dill

1 Halve the eggplant, scoop out the flesh with a sharp knife and chop finely. Salt the insides and leave to drain upside down for 20 minutes while you prepare the other ingredients.

2 Halve the pepper, seed and core. Cut the tops from the tomatoes, scoop out the insides and chop roughly along with the tomato tops.

3 Fry the onion, garlic and chopped eggplant in the oil for 10 minutes, then stir in the rice and cook for 2 minutes.

4 Add the tomato flesh, stock, pine nuts, currants and seasoning. Bring to the boil, cover and simmer for 15 minutes then stir in the fresh herbs.

5 Blanch the eggplant and green pepper halves in boiling water for approximately 3 minutes, then drain them upside down.

6 Spoon the rice filling into all six vegetable "containers" and place on a lightly greased ovenproof shallow dish.

7 Heat the oven to 375°F, drizzle over some olive oil and bake the vegetables for 25–30 minutes. Serve hot, topped with spoonfuls of natural yogurt and dill sprigs.

Red Onion and Zucchini Pizza

It's easy to make a home made pizza using one of the new fast-action yeasts. You can either add the traditional cheese and tomato topping or try something different, such as the one described here.

SERVES 4
3 cups all-purpose flour
1 package fast action/easy blend yeast
2 tsp salt
lukewarm water to mix
TOPPING
2 red onions, thinly sliced
4 tbsp olive oil
2 zucchini, thinly sliced
salt and ground black pepper
fresh nutmeg, grated
4 oz semi-soft goat cheese
6 sun-dried tomatoes in oil, snipped
dried oregano
extra olive oil, to sprinkle

1 Preheat the oven to 400°F. Mix the flour, yeast and salt together, then mix to a firm dough with warm water. How much you will need depends on the flour, but start with ½ cup.

2 Knead the dough for about 5 minutes until it is smooth and elastic, then roll it out to a large circle and place on a lightly greased baking sheet.

3 Set the base aside somewhere warm to rise slightly while you make the topping.

4 Gently fry the onions in half the oil for 5 minutes then add the zucchini and fry for a further 2 minutes. Season and add nutmeg to taste.

5 Spread the pizza base with fried vegetable mixture and dot with the cheese, tomatoes and oregano. Sprinkle over the rest of the olive oil and bake for 12–15 minutes until golden and crisp.

Shepherdess Pie 🍃

A no-meat version of the timeless classic, this dish also has no dairy products in it, so it is suitable for vegans. However, you can serve it with confidence to anyone wanting a hearty meal.

SERVES 6–8
2 lb potatoes
3 tbsp extra virgin olive oil
salt and ground black pepper
1 large onion, chopped
1 green pepper, chopped
2 carrots, coarsely grated
2 garlic cloves
3 tbsp sunflower oil or margarine
4 oz mushrooms, chopped
2 × 14 oz cans aduki beans, drained
2½ cups stock
1 tsp vegetable yeast extract
2 bay leaves
1 tsp dried mixed herbs
dried breadcrumbs or chopped nuts,
   to sprinkle

1 Boil the potatoes in the skins until tender, then drain, reserving a little of the water to moisten them.

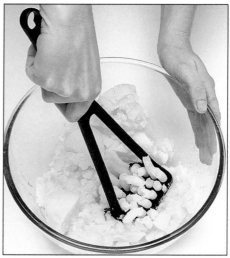

2 Peel the potatoes and mash them well, mixing in the olive oil and seasoning. (Potatoes are easier to peel when boiled in their skins. This also preserves vitamins.)

3 Gently fry the onion, pepper, carrots and garlic in the sunflower oil or margarine for about 5 minutes until they are soft.

4 Stir in the mushrooms and beans and cook for a further 2 minutes, then add the stock, yeast extract, bay leaves and mixed herbs. Simmer for 15 minutes.

5 Remove the bay leaves and empty the vegetables into a shallow ovenproof dish. Spoon on the potatoes in dollops and sprinkle over the crumbs or nuts. Broil until golden brown.

Magnificent Zucchini 🍃

At summer's end, large zucchini –
with their wonderful green and cream
stripes – look so attractive and
tempting. They make delicious,
inexpensive main courses, just right
for a satisfying family Sunday lunch.

SERVES 4–6
3 cups pasta shells
3–4 lb zucchini
1 onion, chopped
1 pepper, seeded and chopped
1 tbsp fresh ginger root, grated
2 garlic cloves, crushed
3 tbsp sunflower oil
4 large tomatoes, skinned and chopped
salt and ground black pepper
½ cup pine nuts
1 tbsp fresh basil, chopped
cheese, grated, to serve (optional)

1 Preheat the oven to 375°F. Boil the
pasta according to the instructions on the
package, slightly overcooking it so that it
is just a little soft. Drain thoroughly and
set to one side.

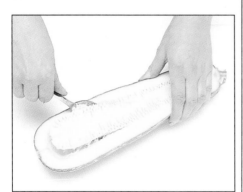

2 Cut the zucchini in half lengthwise
and scoop out the seeds. These can be
discarded. Use a small sharp knife and
tablespoon to scoop out the zucchini
flesh. Chop the flesh roughly.

3 Gently fry the onion, pepper, ginger
and garlic in the oil for 5 minutes then
add the zucchini flesh, tomatoes and
seasoning. Cover and cook for 10–12
minutes until the vegetables are soft.

4 Add to the pan the pasta, pine nuts
and basil, stir well and set aside.

5 Meanwhile, place the zucchini halves
in a roasting pan, season lightly and pour
a little water around the zucchini, taking
care it does not spill inside. Cover with foil
and bake for 15 minutes.

6 Remove the foil, discard the water and
fill the shells with the vegetable mixture.
Re-cover with foil and return to the oven
for a further 20–25 minutes.

7 If you wish, serve this dish topped
with grated cheese. The zucchini can
either be served cut into sections or
scooped out of the "shell."

Turnip and Chick Pea Cobbler

A good mid-week meal with an attractive savory scone topping. Use a star shape cutter for the topping.

SERVES 4–6
1 onion, sliced
2 carrots, chopped
3 medium size turnips, chopped
1 small sweet potato, chopped
2 celery stalks, sliced thinly
3 tbsp sunflower oil
½ tsp ground coriander
½ tsp dried mixed herbs
1 × 15 oz can chopped tomatoes
1 × 14 oz can chick peas
1 vegetable stock cube
salt and ground black pepper
TOPPING
2 cups self-rising flour
1 tsp baking powder
4 tbsp margarine
3 tbsp sunflower seeds
2 tbsp Parmesan cheese, grated
⅔ cup milk

1 Fry all the vegetables in the oil for about 10 minutes until they are soft. Add the coriander, herbs, tomatoes, chick peas with their liquor and stock cube. Season well and simmer for 20 minutes.

2 Pour the vegetables into a shallow casserole dish while you make the topping. Preheat the oven to 375°F.

3 Mix together the flour and baking powder, then rub in the margarine until it resembles fine crumbs. Stir in the seeds and Parmesan cheese. Add the milk and mix to a firm dough.

4 Lightly roll out the topping to a thickness of ½ in and stamp out star shapes or rounds, or simply cut it into small squares.

5 Place the shapes on top of the vegetable mixture and brush with a little extra milk. Bake for 12–15 minutes until risen and golden brown. Serve hot with green, leafy vegetables.

Tangy Fricassé

Vegetables in a light tangy sauce and covered with a crispy crumb topping make a simple and easy main course to serve with crusty bread and salad.

SERVES 4
4 zucchini, sliced
4 oz green beans, sliced
4 large tomatoes, skinned and sliced
1 onion, sliced
4 tbsp butter or sunflower margarine
⅓ cup all-purpose flour
2 tsp coarse grain mustard
2 cups milk
⅔ cup natural yogurt
1 tsp dried thyme
4 oz sharp cheese, grated
salt and ground black pepper
4 tbsp fresh whole wheat bread crumbs
  tossed with 1 tbsp sunflower oil

1 Blanch the zucchini and beans in a small amount of boiling water for just 5 minutes, then drain and arrange in a shallow ovenproof dish.

2 Arrange all but three slices of tomato on top. Put the onion into a saucepan with the butter or margarine and fry gently for 5 minutes.

3 Stir in the flour and mustard, cook for a minute then add the milk gradually until the sauce has thickened. Simmer for a further 2 minutes.

4 Remove the pan from the heat, add the yogurt, thyme and cheese, stirring until melted. Season to taste. Reheat gently if you wish, but do not allow the sauce to boil or it will curdle.

5 Pour the sauce over the vegetables and scatter the bread crumbs on top. Brown under a preheated broiler until golden and crisp, taking care not to let them burn. Garnish with the reserved tomato slices if desired.

Pistachio Pilaf in a Spinach Crown

Saffron and ginger are traditional rice spices and even more delicious when mixed with fresh pistachio nuts. This is a particularly good, light main course needing just a tomato salad for accompaniment.

SERVES 4

3 onions
4 tbsp olive oil
2 garlic cloves, crushed
1 in cube fresh ginger root, grated
1 fresh green chili, chopped
2 carrots, coarsely grated
1¼ cups basmati rice, rinsed
¼ tsp saffron strands, crushed
2 cups stock
1 cinnamon stick
1 tsp ground coriander
salt and ground black pepper
¼ cup fresh pistachio nuts
1 lb fresh leaf spinach, well washed
1 tsp garam masala powder

1 Roughly chop two of the onions. Heat half the oil in a large saucepan and fry the onion with half the garlic, the ginger and the chili for 5 minutes.

2 Mix in the carrots and rice, cook for 1 more minute and then add the saffron, stock, cinnamon and coriander. Season well. Bring to a boil, then cover and simmer gently for 10 minutes, without lifting the lid.

3 Remove from the heat and leave to stand, uncovered, for 5 minutes. Add the pistachio nuts, mixing them in with a fork. Remove the cinnamon stick and keep the rice warm.

4 Thinly slice the third onion and fry in the remaining oil for about 3 minutes. Stir in the spinach. Cover and cook for another 2 minutes.

5 Add the garam masala powder. Cook until just tender then drain and roughly chop the spinach.

6 Spoon the spinach round the edge of a round serving dish and pile the pilaf in the center. Serve hot.

Spinach Bread and Butter Casserole

Ideally, use Italian ciabatta bread for this, or a French style baguette. It makes a much lighter dish.

SERVES 4–6
14 oz fresh leaf spinach
1 ciabatta loaf, thinly sliced
4 tbsp softened butter, olive oil or
  low fat spread
1 red onion, thinly sliced
4 oz mushrooms, thinly sliced
2 tbsp olive oil
1 tsp cumin seeds
salt and ground black pepper
4 oz Gruyère or Gouda cheese, grated
3 eggs
2¼ cups milk
fresh nutmeg, grated

1 Rinse the spinach well and blanch it in the tiniest amount of water for 2 minutes. Drain well, pressing out any excess water, and chop roughly.

2 Spread the bread slices thinly with the butter or low fat spread. Grease a large shallow ovenproof dish and line the base and sides with bread.

3 Fry the onion and mushrooms lightly in the oil for 5 minutes then add the cumin seeds and spinach. Season well.

4 Layer the spinach mixture with the remaining bread and half the cheese. For the top, mix everything together and sprinkle over the remaining cheese.

5 Beat the eggs with the milk, adding seasoning and nutmeg to taste. Pour slowly over the whole dish and set aside for a good hour to allow the custard to be absorbed into the bread.

6 Preheat the oven to 375°F. Stand the dish in a roasting pan and pour around some boiling water for a bain marie. Bake for 40–45 minutes until risen, golden brown and crispy on top.

Mushroom Puffs

If possible, use the fuller-flavored cremini, or brown, mushrooms for these tasty puffs.

MAKES 8
2 × 8 oz blocks frozen puff pastry, thawed
1 egg, beaten
FILLING
1 onion, chopped
1 carrot, coarsely grated
1 medium potato, coarsely grated
3 tbsp sunflower oil
8 oz sliced mushrooms
2 tbsp soy sauce
1 tbsp tomato ketchup
1 tbsp dry sherry (optional)
good pinch dried thyme
salt and ground black pepper

1 Roll out the pastry blocks until they are ¼ in thick and cut each block into four 6 in squares. Reserve a little pastry for decoration. Cover the rolled pastry squares and trimmings and set aside in a cool place to rest.

2 Make the filling by gently frying the onion, carrot and potato in the oil for 5 minutes, then add the mushrooms, soy sauce, ketchup, sherry (if using), thyme and seasoning.

3 Cook, stirring occasionally, until the mushrooms and vegetables have softened and feel quite tender. Cool.

4 Divide the filling between the eight squares, placing it to one side across the diagonal. Brush the pastry edges with egg then fold over into triangles and press well to seal. From the pastry scraps, cut out little shapes, such as mushrooms, to decorate the pasties.

5 Crimp each puff edge and top with the cut-out shapes. Set on two baking sheets. Preheat the oven to 400°F and, in the meantime, allow the puffs to rest somewhere cool.

6 Glaze the puffs with beaten egg, then bake for 15–20 minutes until golden brown and crisp.

Winter Casserole with Herb Dumplings

When the cold weather draws in, gather together a good selection of vegetables and make this comforting casserole with some hearty old-fashioned dumplings.

SERVES 6
2 potatoes
2 carrots
1 small fennel bulb
1 small rutabaga
2 leeks
2 zucchini
4 tbsp butter or margarine
2 tbsp all-purpose flour
1 × 15 oz can lima beans, with liquor
2½ cups stock
2 tbsp tomato paste
1 cinnamon stick
2 tsp ground coriander
½ tsp ground ginger
2 bay leaves
salt and ground black pepper
DUMPLINGS
1½ cups all-purpose flour
4 oz vegetable suet, shredded, or chilled
   butter, grated
1 tsp dried thyme
1 tsp salt
½ cup milk

1 Cut all the vegetables into even, bite size chunks, then fry gently in the butter or margarine for about 10 minutes.

2 Stir in the flour then the liquor from the beans, the stock, tomato paste, spices, bay leaves and seasoning. Bring to a boil, stirring all the time.

3 Cover and simmer for 10 minutes, then add the beans and cook for a further 5 minutes.

4 Meanwhile, to make the dumplings, simply mix the flour, suet or butter, thyme and salt to a firm but moist dough with the milk and knead with your hands until it is smooth.

VARIATION

Try chopped walnuts and grated Parmesan or dumplings *fines herbes*. Finely chop ingredients and stir into flour.

5 Divide the dough into 12 pieces, rolling each one into a ball with your fingers. Uncover the simmering stew and then add the dumplings, allowing space between each one for expansion.

6 Replace the lid and cook on a gentle simmer for a further 15 minutes. Do not peek – or you will let out all the steam. Neither should you cook dumplings too fast, or they will break up. Remove the cinnamon stick and bay leaves before you serve this dish, steaming hot.

Lasagne Rolls

Perhaps a more elegant presentation than ordinary lasagne, but just as tasty and popular. You will need to boil "no-need-to-cook" lasagne as it needs to be soft enough to roll!

SERVES 4
8–10 lasagne sheets
Lentil Bolognese (see below)
8 oz fresh leaf spinach, well washed
4 oz mushrooms, sliced
4 oz Mozzarella cheese, thinly sliced
BECHAMEL SAUCE
scant ½ cup all-purpose flour
3 tbsp butter or margarine
2½ cups milk
bay leaf
salt and ground black pepper
fresh nutmeg, grated
freshly grated Parmesan or Pecorino
  cheese, to serve

1 Cook the lasagne sheets according to instructions on the package, or for about 10 minutes. Drain and allow to cool.

2 Cook the spinach in the tiniest amount of water for 2 minutes then add the sliced mushrooms and cook for a further 2 minutes. Drain very well, pressing out all the excess liquor, and chop roughly.

3 Put all the bechamel ingredients into a saucepan and bring slowly to a boil, stirring continuously until the sauce is thick and smooth. Simmer for 2 minutes with the bay leaf then season well and stir in grated nutmeg to taste.

VARIATION

Needless to say, the fillings in this recipe could be any of your own choice. One of my favorites is a lightly stir-fried mixture of colorful vegetables such as peppers, zucchini, eggplant and mushrooms, topped with a cheese bechamel as above, or with a fresh tomato sauce, which is especially good in summer.

4 Lay out the pasta sheets and spread with the bolognese sauce, spinach and mushrooms and mozzarella. Roll up each one and place in a large shallow casserole dish with the join face down.

5 Remove and discard the bay leaf and then pour the sauce over the pasta. Sprinkle over the cheese and place under a hot broiler to brown.

Lentil Bolognese

A really useful sauce to serve with pasta, such as lasagne rolls, as a crêpe stuffing or even as a protein-packed sauce for vegetables.

SERVES 6
1 onion, chopped
2 garlic cloves, crushed
2 carrots, coarsely grated
2 celery stalks, chopped
3 tbsp olive oil
⅔ cup red lentils
1 × 14 oz can chopped tomatoes
2 tbsp tomato paste
2 cups stock
1 tbsp fresh marjoram, chopped, or
  1 tsp dried marjoram
salt and ground black pepper

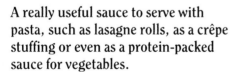

1 In a large saucepan, gently fry the onion, garlic, carrots and celery in the oil for about 5 minutes, until they are soft.

2 Add the lentils, tomatoes, tomato paste, stock, marjoram and seasoning.

3 Bring the mixture to a boil then partially cover with a lid and simmer for 20 minutes until thick and soft. Use the bolognese sauce as required.

Broccoli Risotto Torte

Like a Spanish omelette, this is a savory cake served in wedges. It is good cold or hot, and needs only a salad as an accompaniment.

SERVES 6

8 oz broccoli, cut into very small florets
1 onion, chopped
2 garlic cloves, crushed
1 large yellow pepper, sliced
2 tbsp olive oil
4 tbsp butter
1¼ cups Arborio rice
½ cup dry white wine
4½ cups stock
salt and ground black pepper
4 oz fresh or Parmesan cheese, coarsely
  grated
4 eggs, separated
oil, for greasing
sliced tomato and chopped parsley,
  to garnish

1 Blanch the broccoli for 3 minutes then drain and reserve.

2 In a large saucepan, gently fry the onion, garlic and pepper in the oil and butter for 5 minutes until they are soft.

3 Stir in the rice, cook for a minute then pour in the wine. Cook, stirring the mixture until the liquid is absorbed.

4 Pour in the stock, season well, bring to a boil then lower to a simmer. Cook for 20 minutes, stirring occasionally.

5 Meanwhile, grease a 10 in round deep cake pan and then line the base with a disc of waxed paper. Preheat the oven to 350°F.

6 Stir the cheese into the rice, allow the mixture to cool for 5 minutes, then beat in the egg yolks.

7 Whisk the egg whites until they form soft peaks and carefully fold into the rice. Turn into the prepared pan and bake for about 1 hour until risen, golden brown and slightly wobbly in the center.

8 Allow the torte to cool in the pan, then chill if serving cold. Run a knife round the edge of the pan and shake out onto a serving plate. If liked, garnish with sliced tomato and chopped parsley.

Leek and Chèvre Lasagne

An unusual and lighter than average lasagne using a soft French goat cheese. The pasta sheets are not so chewy if boiled briefly first. If you do choose no-cook lasagne, then make more sauce to soak into the pasta.

SERVES 6
6–8 lasagne pasta sheets
salt
1 large eggplant
3 leeks, thinly sliced
2 tbsp olive oil
2 red peppers, roasted
7 oz Chèvre, broken into pieces
2 oz Pecorino or Parmesan cheese, freshly grated
SAUCE
½ cup all-purpose flour
5 tbsp butter
3¾ cups milk
½ tsp ground bay leaves
fresh nutmeg, grated
ground black pepper

1 Blanch the pasta sheets in plenty of boiling water for just 2 minutes. Drain and place on a clean dish towel.

2 Lightly salt the eggplant and lay in a colander to drain for 30 minutes, then rinse and pat dry with paper towel.

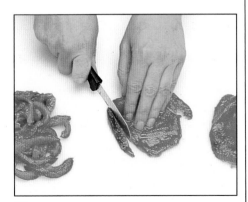

3 Lightly fry the leeks in the oil for about 5 minutes until softened. Peel the roasted peppers and cut into strips.

4 Make the sauce: put the flour, butter and milk into a saucepan and bring to a boil, stirring constantly until it has thickened. Add the ground bay leaves, nutmeg and seasoning. Simmer for a further 2 minutes.

5 In a greased shallow casserole, layer the leeks, pasta, eggplant, Chèvre and Pecorino or Parmesan. Trickle the sauce over the layers, ensuring that plenty goes in between.

6 Finish with a layer of sauce and grated cheese. Bake in the oven at 375°F for 30 minutes or until browned on top. Serve the lasagne immediately.

Glamorgan Sausages

An old Welsh recipe which tastes particularly good served with creamy mashed potatoes and lightly cooked green cabbage.

SERVES 4

2 cups fresh whole wheat bread crumbs
6 oz sharp Cheddar or Caerphilly
  cheese, grated
2 tbsp leek or scallion, finely chopped
2 tbsp fresh parsley, chopped
1 tbsp fresh marjoram, chopped
1 tbsp coarse grain mustard
2 eggs, 1 separated
ground black pepper
½ cup dried bread crumbs
oil, for deep fat frying

1 Mix the fresh bread crumbs with the cheese, leek or scallion, parsley, marjoram, mustard, whole egg, one egg yolk and black pepper to taste. The mixture may appear dry at first but if you knead it lightly it will come together. Make 8 small sausage shapes.

2 Whisk the egg white until lightly frothy and put the dried bread crumbs into a bowl. Dip the sausages first into egg white, and then coat them evenly in breadcrumbs, shaking off any excess.

3 Heat a deep fat frying pan a third full of oil and carefully fry four sausages at a time for 2 minutes each. Drain on paper towel and reheat the oil to repeat.

4 Keep the sausages warm in the oven, uncovered. Alternatively, open freeze, bag and seal, then to reheat, thaw for 1 hour and cook in a moderately hot oven for 10–15 minutes.

Brazilian Stuffed Peppers

Colorful and full of flavor, these stuffed peppers are easy to make in advance. They can be reheated quickly in a microwave oven and browned under a broiler.

SERVES 4

4 peppers, halved and seeded
1 eggplant, cut in chunks
1 onion, sliced
1 garlic clove, crushed
2 tbsp olive oil
1 × 14 oz can chopped tomatoes
1 tsp ground coriander
salt and ground black pepper
1 tbsp fresh basil, chopped
4 oz goat cheese, coarsely crumbled
2 tbsp dried bread crumbs

1 Blanch the pepper halves in boiling water for 3 minutes, then drain well.

2 Sprinkle the eggplant chunks with salt, place in a colander and leave to drain for 20 minutes. Rinse and pat dry.

3 Fry the onion and garlic in the oil for 5 minutes until they are soft, then add the eggplant and cook for a further 5 minutes, stirring occasionally.

VARIATION

There are all sorts of delicious stuffings for peppers. Rice or pasta make a good base, mixed with some lightly fried onion, garlic and spices. Mixed nuts, finely chopped, can be added and a beaten egg or grated cheese helps to bind it all together. Vegans can leave out the last two ingredients.

4 Pour in the tomatoes, coriander and seasoning. Bring to a boil, then simmer for 10 minutes until the mixture is thick. Cool slightly, stir in the basil and half of the cheese.

5 Spoon into the pepper halves and place on a shallow heatproof serving dish. Sprinkle with cheese and bread crumbs, then brown lightly under the broiler. Serve with rice and salad.

Couscous-stuffed Cabbage

A whole stuffed cabbage makes a wonderful main dish, especially for a Sunday lunch. It can be made ahead and steamed when required. Cut into wedges and serve accompanied by a fresh tomato or cheese sauce or even a vegetarian gravy.

SERVES 4
1 medium size cabbage
1 cup couscous grains
1 onion, chopped
1 small red pepper, chopped
2 garlic cloves, crushed
2 tbsp olive oil
1 tsp ground coriander
½ tsp ground cumin
good pinch ground cinnamon
½ cup green lentils, soaked
2½ cups stock
2 tbsp tomato paste
salt and ground black pepper
2 tbsp fresh parsley, chopped
2 tbsp pine nuts or flaked almonds
3 oz sharp Cheddar cheese, grated
1 egg, beaten

1 Cut the top quarter off the cabbage and remove any loose outer leaves. Using a small sharp knife, cut out as much of the middle as you can. Reserve a few larger leaves for later.

2 Blanch the cabbage in a pan of boiling water for 5 minutes, then drain it well, upside down.

VARIATION

You could substitute healthy brown rice for the couscous.

3 Steam the couscous according to the instructions on the package, ensuring that the grains are light and fluffy.

4 Lightly fry the onion, pepper and garlic in the oil for 5 minutes until soft then stir in the spices and cook for a further 2 minutes.

5 Add the lentils and pour in the stock and tomato paste. Bring to a boil, season and simmer for 25 minutes until the lentils are cooked.

6 Mix in the couscous, parsley, nuts or almonds, cheese and egg. Check the seasoning again. Open up the cabbage and spoon in the stuffing.

7 Blanch the leftover outer cabbage leaves and place these over the top of the stuffing, then wrap the whole cabbage in a sheet of buttered foil.

8 Place in a steamer over simmering water and cook for about 45 minutes. Remove from the foil and serve cut into wedges.

Couscous Aromatique

The cuisine of Morocco and Tunisia has many wonderful dishes using the wheat grain couscous which is steamed over simmering spicy stews. A little of the fiery harissa paste stirred in at the end adds an extra zing.

SERVES 4–6
1 lb couscous grains
4 tbsp olive oil
1 onion, cut in chunks
2 carrots, cut in thick slices
4 baby turnips, halved
8 small new potatoes, halved
1 green pepper, cut in chunks
4 oz green beans, halved
1 small fennel bulb, sliced thickly
1 in cube fresh ginger root, grated
2 garlic cloves, crushed
1 tsp ground turmeric
1 tbsp ground coriander
1 tsp cumin seeds
1 tsp ground cinnamon
3 tbsp red lentils
1 × 14 oz can chopped tomatoes
4½ cups stock
4 tbsp raisins
salt and ground black pepper
rind and juice of 1 lemon
harissa paste, to serve (optional)

1 Cover the couscous with cold water and soak for 10 minutes. Drain and spread out on a tray for 20 minutes, stirring it occasionally with your fingers.

2 Meanwhile, in a large saucepan, heat the oil and fry the vegetables for about 10 minutes, stirring from time to time.

3 Add the ginger, garlic and spices, stir well and cook for 2 minutes. Pour in the lentils, tomatoes, stock and raisins, and add seasoning.

4 Bring to a boil, then turn down to a simmer. By this time the couscous should be ready for steaming. Place in a steamer and fit this on top of the stew.

5 Cover and steam gently for about 20 minutes. The grains should be swollen and soft. Fork through and season well. Spoon into a serving dish.

6 Add the lemon rind and juice to the stew and check the seasoning. If liked, add harissa paste to taste; it is quite hot so beware! Serve the stew from a casserole dish separately. Spoon the couscous onto a plate and ladle the stew on top.

SALADS
&
VEGETABLE DISHES

Here is a delightful range of colorful salads and delicious
vegetable dishes and accompaniments. Varied but easy to obtain
ingredients ensure the perfect recipe for every style of meal.

Useful Dressings

A good dressing can make even the simplest combination of fresh vegetables a memorable treat. Remember, in addition to normal salads, lightly cooked hot vegetables such as carrots and potatoes or pulses and grains absorb more flavor and are less greasy if dressed while hot.

Home made Mayonnaise
Make this by hand, if possible. If you make it in a food processor, it will be noticeably lighter.

---

2 egg yolks
½ tsp salt
½ tsp dry mustard
ground black pepper
1¼ cups sunflower oil, or half olive
    and half sunflower oil
1 tbsp wine vinegar
1 tbsp hot water

1 Put the yolks into a bowl with the salt and mustard and a grinding of pepper.

2 Stand the bowl on a damp dish cloth. Using a whisk, beat the yolks and the seasoning thoroughly, then beat in a small trickle of oil.

3 Continue trickling in the oil, adding it in very small amounts. The secret of a good, thick mayonnaise is to add the oil very slowly, beating each addition well before you add more. When all the oil is added, mix in the vinegar and hot water.

To make mayonnaise in a blender, use one whole egg and one yolk instead of two yolks. Blend the eggs with the seasonings. Then, with the blades running, trickle in the oil very slowly. Add the vinegar.

Original Thousand Islands Dressing

---

4 tbsp sunflower oil
1 tbsp fresh orange juice
1 tbsp fresh lemon juice
2 tsp grated lemon rind
1 tbsp finely chopped onion
1 tsp paprika
1 tsp Worcestershire sauce
1 tbsp finely chopped parsley
salt and ground black pepper

Put all the ingredients into a screw top jar, season to taste and shake vigorously. Great with green salads, grated carrot and hot potato, pasta and rice salads.

Yogurt Dressing

⅔ cup natural yogurt
2 tbsp mayonnaise
2 tbsp milk
1 tbsp fresh parsley, chopped
1 tbsp fresh chives or scallions, chopped
salt and ground black pepper

Simply mix all the ingredients together thoroughly in a bowl.

Peperonata with Raisins

Sliced roasted peppers in dressing with vinegar-soaked raisins make a tasty side salad which complements many other dishes and is quick to make, especially if you already have a batch of peppers in oil.

SERVES 2–4
6 tbsp sliced red or green peppers
   in olive oil, drained
1 tbsp onion, chopped
2 tbsp balsamic vinegar
3 tbsp raisins
2 tbsp fresh parsley, chopped
ground black pepper

1 Toss the peppers with the onion and leave to steep for an hour.

2 Put the vinegar and raisins in a small saucepan and heat for a minute, then allow to cool.

3 Mix all the ingredients together thoroughly and spoon into a serving bowl. Serve lightly chilled.

VARIATION

Peperonata is one of the classic Italian antipasto dishes, served at the start of each meal with crusty bread to mop up the delicious juices. Try serving shavings of fresh Parmesan cheese alongside, or buy a good selection of green and black olives to accompany the peperonata. Small baby tomatoes will complete the antipasto.

Mighty Mushrooms

There is now a wide variety of cultivated mushrooms on sale in larger supermarkets and greengrocers so a simple side dish of mushrooms becomes quite exciting. This also makes an excellent sauce to serve tossed into pasta. Dried ceps or porcini mushrooms are on sale in delicatessens if you have trouble finding them in supermarkets.

SERVES 4
½ oz package dried porcini mushrooms/ceps (optional)
4 tbsp olive oil
8 oz button mushrooms, halved or sliced
4 oz oyster mushrooms
4 oz fresh shiitake mushrooms, or 1 oz dried and soaked mushrooms
2 garlic cloves, crushed
2 tsp ground coriander
salt and ground black pepper
3 tbsp fresh parsley, chopped

1 If you are using porcini mushrooms (and they do give a good rich flavor), soak them in a little hot water just to cover for 20 minutes.

2 In a large saucepan, heat the oil and add all the mushrooms, including the soaked porcinis, if using. Stir well, cover and cook gently for 5 minutes.

3 Stir in the garlic, coriander and seasoning. Cook for another 5 minutes until the mushrooms are tender and much of the liquor has been reduced.

4 Mix in the parsley, allow to cool slightly and serve.

Tomato Sauce

A basic sauce which can either be part of a larger recipe or served as a side sauce. For extra flavor, add red pepper, or vary the taste with orange rind and juice, chopped fresh herbs such as basil, or spice it up with some chili sauce.

SERVES 4–6
1 onion, chopped
2 garlic cloves, crushed
1 small red pepper (optional), chopped
3 tbsp olive oil
1½ lb fresh tomatoes, skinned and chopped, or 1 × 14 oz can chopped tomatoes
1 tsp granulated sugar
salt and ground black pepper
2 tbsp fresh herbs, chopped, e.g. basil, parsley, marjoram (optional)

1 Gently fry the onion, garlic and red pepper, if using, in the oil for 5 minutes until they are soft.

2 Stir in the tomatoes, add the sugar and seasoning to taste, bring to a boil then cover and simmer for 15–20 minutes.

3 The sauce should now be thick and pulpy. If it is a little thin, then boil it – uncovered – so that it reduces down. Stir in the fresh herbs, if using, and then check the seasoning.

COOK'S TIP

Why not make up a large batch of this sauce and freeze it in two-portion sizes?

Stir-fried Cabbage

An often under-rated vegetable, crisp cabbage is wonderful when lightly cooked the Chinese way in a wok. Any cabbage will do, but perhaps the Savoy cabbage is the nicest.

SERVES 4
½ small cabbage
2 tbsp sunflower oil
1 tbsp light soy sauce
1 tbsp fresh lemon juice (optional)
2 tsp caraway seeds
ground black pepper

1 Cut the central core from the cabbage, and shred the leaves finely.

2 Heat the oil until quite hot in a wok and then stir-fry the cabbage for about 2 minutes.

3 Toss in the soy sauce, lemon juice, if using, caraway seeds and pepper, to taste.

Perfect Creamed Potatoes

If a bowl of plain, mashed potatoes sounds boring, then try serving it this way – in the French style.

SERVES 4
2 lb potatoes, peeled and diced
3 tbsp extra virgin olive oil
about ⅔ cup hot milk
fresh nutmeg, grated
salt and ground black pepper
a few leaves fresh basil or sprigs fresh parsley, chopped

1 Boil the potatoes until just tender and not too mushy. Drain very well. Ideally press the potatoes through a special potato "ricer" (rather like a large garlic press) or mash them well with a potato masher. Do not pass them through a food processor or you will have a gluey mess.

2 Beat the olive oil into the potato and mix in just enough hot milk to make a smooth, thick purée.

3 Flavor to taste with the nutmeg and seasoning, then stir in the fresh chopped herbs. Spoon into a warm serving dish and serve as soon as possible.

COOK'S TIP

Choosing the right potato makes all the difference to creamed or mashed potatoes. A waxy variety won't be light and fluffy, and a potato which breaks down too quickly on boiling will become a slurry when mashed. Most bags of potatoes carry guidelines on what method of cooking they are suited for. In general, red potatoes will make a good mash, as will Florida Creamers and Yukon Golds.

Oven Chip Roasties

Very popular with children and a much better alternative for all the family to high fat roast potatoes.

SERVES 4–6
4 medium to large baking potatoes
⅔ cup olive oil
1 tsp dried mixed herbs (optional)
sea salt flakes

1 Preheat the oven to the highest possible temperature, generally 450°F. Place a lightly oiled roasting pan in the oven to get really hot.

2 Cut the potatoes in half lengthwise, then into long thin wedges. Brush each side lightly with oil.

3 When the oven is really hot, remove the pan carefully and scatter the potato slices over it in a single layer.

4 Sprinkle the potatoes with the herbs and salt and place in the oven for about 20 minutes or until they are golden brown, crisp and lightly puffy. Serve immediately.

VARIATION

Parsnips also make fine oven chips. Choose large parsnips which tend to have more flavor. Slice thinly on a diagonal and roast in the same way as above, although you may find they do not take as long to cook. They make great mid-week suppers for kids and grown-ups served with fried eggs, mushrooms and tomatoes.

Warm Spicy Dhal

If you thought split yellow peas were only for soups, then try this Indian inspired dish. Serve with rice, chappatis or naan bread and whatever main dish you like – perhaps eggs, fried eggplant, or even a tasty dish of fried mushrooms.

SERVES 4–6
8 oz yellow split peas
2 onions, chopped
1 large bay leaf
2½ cups stock or water
salt and ground black pepper
2 tsp black mustard seeds
2 tbsp butter, melted
1 garlic clove, crushed
1 in cube fresh ginger root, grated
1 small green pepper, sliced
1 tsp ground turmeric
1 tsp garam masala or mild curry powder
3 tomatoes, skinned and chopped
fresh coriander or parsley, to serve

1 Put the split peas, 1 onion and the bay leaf in the stock or water, in a covered pan. Simmer for 25 minutes, seasoning lightly towards the end.

2 In a separate pan, fry the mustard seeds in the butter for about 30 seconds until they start to pop, then add all the remaining onion, along with the garlic, ginger and green pepper.

3 Sauté for about 5 minutes until softened, then stir in the remaining spices and fry for a few seconds more.

4 Add the split peas, tomatoes, and a little extra water if it needs it. Cover and simmer for a further 10 minutes, then check the seasoning and serve hot garnished with coriander or parsley.

Peas and Lettuce

Do not discard the tough, outer leaves of lettuce – they are delicious if shredded and cooked with peas.

SERVES 4
6 outer leaves of lettuce, e.g. Boston, Cobb
1 small onion or shallot, sliced
2 tbsp butter or sunflower margarine
8 oz fresh or frozen peas
fresh nutmeg, grated
salt and ground black pepper

1 Pull off the outer lettuce leaves and wash them well. Roughly shred the leaves with your hands.

2 In a saucepan, lightly fry the lettuce and onion or shallot in the butter or margarine for 3 minutes.

3 Add the peas, nutmeg to taste and seasoning. Stir, cover and simmer for about 5 minutes. This dish can be drained or served slightly wet.

Hash Browns

A traditional American breakfast dish, hash browns can be served any time of day. They are a tasty way of using up any leftover boiled potatoes.

SERVES 4
4 tbsp sunflower or olive oil
1 lb cooked potatoes, diced
1 small onion, chopped
salt and ground black pepper

1 Heat the oil in a large, heavy-based frying pan and when quite hot add the potatoes in a single layer. Scatter the onion on top and season well.

2 Cook on a moderate heat until browned underneath, pressing down on the potatoes with a spoon or spatula to squash them together.

3 When the potatoes are nicely browned, turn them over in sections with a spatula and fry on the other side, pressing them down once again. Serve when heated through and lightly crispy.

Brussels Sprouts Stir-fry

Brussels sprouts are delicious when quickly stir-fried – they are really full-flavored and their texture is full of crisp bite. Small Brussels sprouts have the best flavor.

SERVES 6

2 tbsp groundnut or sunflower oil
1 lb small Brussels sprouts, trimmed and halved
3 scallions, sliced
2 garlic cloves, crushed
1 small yellow pepper, sliced
2 tbsp light soy sauce
1 tbsp sesame seed oil
good pinch of granulated sugar
ground black pepper
2 tbsp sesame seeds, toasted

1 Heat the oil in a wok until quite hot, then stir-fry the sprouts for 2 minutes.

2 Add the scallions, garlic and yellow pepper and fry for another 2 minutes, stirring all the time.

3 Toss in the soy sauce, sesame seed oil, sugar, and season with pepper. Scatter over the sesame seeds and then serve immediately.

Hassleback Potatoes

These rather splendid roast potatoes are ideal to serve for dinner parties or special occasions such as Christmas. Use a good quality baking potato for the best results.

SERVES 4
olive or sunflower oil, for roasting
4 medium potatoes, peeled and halved
   lengthwise
salt and ground black pepper
1 tbsp plain white or whole wheat dried
   bread crumbs

1 Pour enough oil into a small roasting pan just to cover the base then put into an oven set at 400°F to heat.

2 Meanwhile, par boil the potato halves for 5 minutes then drain. Cool slightly and slash about four times from the rounded tops almost down to the flat bottoms.

3 Place the potatoes in the heated roasting pan and spoon over the hot oil. Season well and return the potatoes to the oven for about 20 minutes.

4 Remove the potatoes once more from the oven, prise open the slashes slightly and baste with the hot oil. Sprinkle the potato tops lightly with bread crumbs and return to the oven for another 15 minutes or so until they are golden brown, cooked and crispy.

COOK'S TIP

There are many different ways of roasting potatoes in the oven. First, the choice of potato is important. Choose a variety which holds its shape well and yet is still slightly floury inside. Details on the package or bag should give you guidance. The oil is important too – choose one which is either flavorless such as sunflower or groundnut oil or one with a lot of good flavor, such as olive oil. Just before serving, try trickling a little sesame seed, walnut or hazelnut oil over the roasted potatoes for a delicious nutty flavor.

PARTIES & PICNICS

From informal meals, ideal for outdoor entertaining, to elegant and
delicious dishes that will add style to special occasions, here are
recipes to suit every festivity.

Grilled Vegetables with Salsa

Enjoy a barbecue with these chunky grilled vegetables. Serve hot with a no-cook salsa.

SERVES 4
1 large sweet potato, cut in thick slices
2 zucchini, halved lengthwise
salt
2 red peppers, quartered
olive oil, to brush
SALSA
2 large tomatoes, skinned and finely chopped
2 scallions, finely chopped
1 small green chili, chopped
juice of 1 small lime
2 tbsp fresh coriander, chopped
salt and ground black pepper

1 Par boil the sweet potato for 5 minutes until it is barely tender. Drain thoroughly and leave to cool.

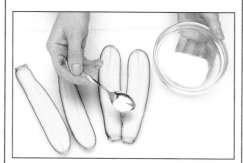

2 Sprinkle the zucchini with a little salt and leave to drain in a colander for 20 minutes, then pat dry.

3 Make the salsa by mixing all the ingredients together, and allow them to stand for about 30 minutes to mellow.

4 Prepare the barbecue until the coals glow, or preheat a broiler. Brush the potato slices, zucchini and peppers with oil and cook them until they are lightly charred and softened, brushing with oil again and turning at least once. Serve hot accompanied by the salsa.

Garden Vegetable Terrine

Perfect for a special family picnic or buffet, this is a softly set, creamy terrine of colorful vegetables wrapped in glossy spinach leaves. Select large, really fresh spinach leaves for the best results.

SERVES 6
8 oz fresh leaf spinach, well washed
3 carrots, cut in sticks
3–4 long, thin leeks
4 oz long green beans, topped and tailed
1 red pepper, cut in strips
2 zucchini, cut in sticks
4 oz broccoli florets
SAUCE
1 egg and 2 yolks
1¼ cups light cream
fresh nutmeg, grated
1 tsp salt
2 oz Cheddar cheese, grated
oil, for greasing
ground black pepper

1 Blanch the spinach quickly in boiling water, then drain, refresh in cold water and drain again. Take care not to break up the leaves, then carefully pat them dry.

2 Grease a 2 lb loaf pan and line the base with a sheet of waxed paper. Line the pan with the spinach leaves, trimming any thick stalks. Allow the leaves to overhang the sides of the pan.

3 Blanch the rest of the vegetables in boiling, salted water until just tender. Drain and refresh in cold water then, when completely cool, pat dry with pieces of paper towel.

4 Place the vegetables into the loaf pan in a colorful mixture, making sure the sticks of vegetables lie lengthwise.

5 Beat the sauce ingredients together and slowly pour over the vegetables. Tap the loaf pan to ensure the sauce seeps into the gaps. Fold over the spinach leaves at the top of the terrine.

6 Cover the terrine with a sheet of greased foil, then bake in a roasting pan half full of boiling water at 350°F for about 1–1¼ hours until set.

7 Cool the terrine in the pan, then chill. To serve, loosen the sides and shake gently out. Serve cut in thick slices.

Tofu Satay

Grill cubes of tofu until crispy, then serve with a Thai-style peanut sauce. Soaking the sticks helps them withstand the hot broiling.

SERVES 4–6
2 × 7 oz packages smoked tofu
3 tbsp light soy sauce
2 tsp sesame oil
1 garlic clove, crushed
1 yellow and 1 red pepper, cut in squares
8–12 fresh bay leaves
sunflower oil, for grilling
SAUCE
2 scallions, finely chopped
2 garlic cloves, crushed
good pinch chili powder or few drops hot chili sauce
1 tsp granulated sugar
1 tbsp white vinegar
2 tbsp light soy sauce
3 tbsp crunchy peanut butter

1 Soak 8–12 wooden satay sticks in water for 20 minutes, then drain. Cut the tofu into bite-sized cubes and mix with the soy sauce, sesame oil and garlic. Cover and marinate for 20 minutes.

2 Beat the sauce ingredients together until well blended. Avoid using a food processor for this as the texture should be slightly chunky.

3 Drain the tofu and thread the cubes onto the soaked sticks with the pepper squares and bay leaves. Larger leaves may need to be halved.

4 Heat a broiler or barbecue until quite hot. Brush the satays with oil. Broil, turning the sticks occasionally, until the ingredients are browned and crisp. Serve hot with the dipping sauce.

Party Mousakka

Always a popular favorite for both guests and the cook at parties, mousakka is ideal because it benefits from being made ahead of time, requiring just reheating on the day.

SERVES 8
2 large eggplants, thinly sliced
6 zucchini, cut in chunks
⅔ cup olive oil, plus extra if required
1½ lb potatoes, thinly sliced
2 onions, sliced
3 garlic cloves, crushed
⅔ cup dry white wine
2 × 14 oz cans chopped tomatoes
2 tbsp tomato paste
1 × 15 oz can green lentils
2 tsp dried oregano
4 tbsp chopped fresh parsley
2 cups feta cheese, crumbled
salt and ground black pepper
BECHAMEL SAUCE
3 tbsp butter
4 tbsp all-purpose flour
2½ cups milk
2 eggs, beaten
4 tbsp freshly grated Parmesan cheese
nutmeg, freshly grated

1 Lightly salt the eggplants and zucchini in a colander and leave them to drain for 30 minutes. Rinse and pat dry.

2 Heat the oil until quite hot in a frying pan and quickly brown the eggplant and zucchini slices. Remove them with a slotted spoon and drain on a paper towel. This step is important to cut down on the oiliness of the eggplant. Next, brown the potato slices, remove and pat dry. Add the onion and garlic to the pan with a little extra oil, if required, and fry until lightly browned – about 5 minutes.

3 Pour in the wine and cook until reduced down then add the tomatoes and lentils plus the liquor from the can. Stir in the herbs and season well. Cover and simmer for 15 minutes.

4 In a large ovenproof dish, layer the vegetables, trickling the tomato and lentil sauce in between and scattering over the feta cheese. Finish off with a layer of eggplant slices.

5 Cover the vegetables with a sheet of foil and bake at 375°F for 25 minutes or until the vegetables are quite soft but not overcooked.

6 Meanwhile, for the bechamel sauce, put the butter, flour and milk into a saucepan all together and bring slowly to a boil, stirring or whisking constantly. It should thicken and become smooth. Season and add the nutmeg.

7 Remove the sauce and cool for 5 minutes then beat in the eggs. Pour it over the eggplant and sprinkle with the Parmesan. If cooking ahead, cool and chill at this stage.

8 To finish, return to the oven uncovered and bake for a further 25–30 minutes until golden and bubbling hot.

Persian Rice and Lentils with a Tahdeeg

Persian or Iranian cuisine is an exotic and delicious one, steeped in history. Flavors are intense and exotic, and somehow more sophisticated than other Mediterranean styles. A tahdeeg is the glorious, golden rice crust that forms at the bottom of the saucepan.

SERVES 8
1 lb basmati rice, rinsed thoroughly and soaked
2 onions, 1 chopped, 1 thinly sliced
2 garlic cloves, crushed
⅔ cup sunflower oil
1 cup green lentils, soaked
2½ cups stock
⅓ cup raisins
2 tsp ground coriander
3 tbsp tomato paste
salt and ground black pepper
few strands of saffron
1 egg yolk, beaten
2 tsp natural yogurt
6 tbsp butter, melted and strained
extra oil, for frying

1 Boil the rinsed and drained rice in plenty of well salted water for 3 minutes only. Drain again.

2 Meanwhile, fry the chopped onion and garlic in 2 tbsp of oil for 5 minutes, then add the lentils, stock, raisins, coriander, tomato paste and seasoning. Bring to a boil, then cover and simmer for 20 minutes. Set aside.

3 Soak the saffron strands in a little hot water. Remove about 8 tbsp of the rice and mix with the egg yolk and yogurt. Season well.

4 In a large saucepan, heat about two-thirds of the remaining oil and scatter the egg and yogurt rice evenly over the base.

5 Scatter the remaining rice into the pan, alternating it with the lentils. Build up in a pyramid shape away from the sides of the pan, finishing with plain rice on top.

6 With a long wooden spoon handle, make three holes down to the bottom of the pan and drizzle over the butter. Bring to a high heat, then wrap the pan lid in a clean, wet dish towel and place firmly on top. When a good head of steam appears, turn the heat down to low. Cook for about 30 minutes.

7 Meanwhile, fry the sliced onion in the remaining oil until browned and crisp. Drain well and set aside.

8 Remove the rice pan from the heat, still covered and stand it briefly in a sink of cold water for a minute or two to loosen the base. Remove the lid and mix a few spoons of the white rice with the saffron water prepared in Step 3.

9 Toss the rice and lentils together in the pan and spoon out onto a serving dish in a mound. Scatter the saffron rice on top. Break up the rice crust on the bottom (the prized tahdeeg) and place around the mound. Scatter the onions on top of the saffron rice and serve.

Birds' Nests

A recipe from an old hand-written cookbook dated 1887. These are also known as *Welsh Eggs* because they resemble Scotch Eggs but they have leeks in the filling. They are ideal for taking on picnics.

SERVES 6
6 eggs, hard-boiled
all-purpose flour for dredging, seasoned with salt and paprika
1 leek, chopped
2 tsp sunflower oil
2 cups fresh white breadcrumbs
grated rind and juice of 1 lmeon
½ cup vegetarian shredded suet
4 tbsp fresh parsley, chopped
1 tsp dried thyme
salt and ground black pepper
1 egg, beaten
½ cup dried breadcrumbs
oil, for deep fat frying
lettuce and tomato slices, to garnish

1 Peel the hard-boiled eggs and toss in the seasoned flour.

2 Fry the leeks in the oil for about 3 minutes. Remove, cool, then mix with the fresh breadcrumbs, lemon rind and juice, suet, herbs and seasoning. If the mixture is somewhat dry add a little water.

3 Shape the mixture around the eggs, then toss first into the beaten egg, then the dried breadcrumbs. Set aside on a plate to chill for 30 minutes.

4 Pour enough oil to fill one-third of a deep fat fryer and heat to a temperature of 375°F, and fry the eggs, three at a time, for about 3 minutes. Remove and drain on paper towel.

5 Serve, cool, cut in half on a platter lined with lettuce and garnished with tomato slices.

Portable Salads

A clever Victorian notion for transporting saucy salads neatly to a picnic site was to pack them in a hollowed out loaf of bread.

SERVES 6
1 large, deep crusty loaf of bread
softened butter or margarine, for
  spreading
few leaves of crisp lettuce
4 eggs, hardboiled and chopped
12 oz new potatoes, boiled and sliced
1 green pepper, thinly sliced
2 carrots, coarsely grated
3 scallions, chopped
4 oz Gouda cheese, grated
salt and ground black pepper
DRESSING
2 tbsp mayonnaise
2 tbsp natural yogurt
2 tbsp milk
1 garlic clove, crushed (optional)
1 tbsp fresh dill, chopped

1 Cut the top from the loaf and scoop out the bread inside. Use this for making fresh bread crumbs and freeze for later.

2 Spread the inside of the loaf lightly with the softened butter or margarine, then line with the lettuce leaves.

3 Mix the eggs with the vegetables and cheese. Season well. Beat the dressing ingredients together and mix into the egg and vegetables.

4 Spoon the dressed salad into the hollow and lined loaf, replace the lid and wrap in plastic wrap. Chill until ready to transport. To serve, spoon the salad onto plates and cut the crust into chunks.

Pan Bagna

You need three essential elements for this French picnic classic: a really fresh French baguette, ripe juicy tomatoes, full of flavor and good, extra virgin olive oil. It is ideal to pack for a picnic.

SERVES 3–4
1 long French baguette, split in half
1 garlic clove, halved
4–6 tbsp extra virgin olive oil
3–4 ripe tomatoes, thinly sliced
salt and ground black pepper
1 small green pepper, thinly sliced
2 oz Gruyère cheese, thinly sliced
a few pitted black olives, sliced
6 fresh basil leaves

1 Rub the cut surface of the bread with the garlic and discard the clove. Brush over half of the olive oil on both halves of the bread.

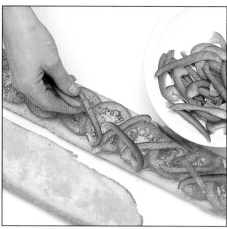

2 Lay the tomato slices on top, season well and top with the pepper. Drizzle over the remaining oil.

3 Top the tomatoes with the cheese slices, olives and basil leaves. Sandwich the loaf together firmly and wrap it in plastic wrap for an hour or more. Serve cut diagonally in thick slices.

Sandwiches, Rolls and Fillings

There is an increasing variety of wonderful breads and rolls now for the picnic packer to choose from – not only variations on white and whole wheat breads, but also flavored breads such as onion, walnut, tomato swirl and black olive. Make sure the breads are fresh and spread them right up to the edges using good butter or a quality margarine spread. Once filled, wrap in plastic wrap and chill until required. However, many a good sandwich is spoiled if served too cold, so allow it to return to room temperature before eating.

FILLING IDEAS
Unless specified, keep the fillings in separate layers rather than mixing the ingredients together.

☐ De-rinded Brie or Camembert, mixed with chopped walnuts or pecans and served with frisé or curly endive lettuce.

☐ Yeast extract, scrambled egg (made without milk) and bean sprout (especially good with alfalfa sprouts). Spread the bread or roll with yeast extract rather than mixing it into the egg.

☐ Fry onions in olive oil until crisp and brown. Cool. Layer with shredded, young raw spinach leaves and grated cheese mixed with a little mayonnaise.

☐ **Real English Cucumber Sandwiches.** Peel strips from a whole cucumber to leave it stripy, then slice thinly on a mandoline or a food processor slicer. Sprinkle lightly with salt and leave to drain for 30 minutes in a colander. Pat dry. Sprinkle lightly with a little vinegar and black pepper. Sandwich in very fresh white or whole wheat bread and cut off the crusts. Cut into small triangles.

DESSERTS & BREADS

Freshly baked breads, cakes and fruit-filled desserts are all utterly irresistible. Here you can also find traditional treats to make Christmas extra special.

Zucchini Crown Bread

Adding grated zucchini and cheese to a loaf mixture will keep it tasting fresher for longer. This is a good loaf to serve with a bowl of special soup.

SERVES 8
1 lb zucchini, coarsely grated
salt
5 cups all-purpose flour
2 packages fast action yeast
4 tbsp Parmesan cheese, freshly grated
ground black pepper
2 tbsp olive oil
lukewarm water, to mix
milk, to glaze
sesame seeds, to garnish

1 Spread out the zucchini in a colander and sprinkle lightly with salt. Leave to drain for 30 minutes, then pat dry.

2 Mix the flour, yeast and Parmesan together and season with black pepper.

3 Stir in the oil and zucchini and add enough lukewarm water to give you a good firm dough.

4 Knead the dough on a lightly floured surface until it is smooth, then return it to the mixing bowl, cover it with oiled plastic wrap and leave it to rise in a warm place.

5 Meanwhile, grease and line a 9 in round cake pan, and then preheat the oven to 400°F.

6 When the dough has doubled in size, turn it out of the bowl, punch it down and knead it lightly. Break into eight balls, rolling each one and placing them in the tin as shown. Brush the tops with milk and sprinkle over the sesame seeds.

7 Allow to rise again, then bake for 25 minutes or until golden brown. Cool slightly in the pan, then turn out the bread to cool further.

Rosemary Focaccia

Italian flat bread is becoming increasingly popular and is easy to make using packaged bread mix. Add traditional ingredients like olives and sun-dried tomatoes.

SERVES 4
1 lb package white bread mix
4 tbsp extra virgin olive oil
2 tsp dried rosemary, crushed
8 sun-dried tomatoes, snipped
12 black olives, pitted and chopped
¾ cup lukewarm water
sea salt flakes

VARIATION

If you want to make your own bread instead of using a bread mix, then use a packet of easy-blend yeast for each 6 cups of flour. Mix the yeast and flour together then add the remaining ingredients as per the recipe.

1 Mix the bread mix with half the oil, the rosemary, tomatoes, olives and water until it forms a firm dough.

2 Turn out the dough onto a lightly floured surface and knead thoroughly for 5 minutes. Return the dough to the mixing bowl and cover with a piece of oiled plastic wrap.

3 Leave the dough to rise in a warm place until it has doubled in size. Meanwhile, lightly grease two baking sheets with olive oil and preheat the oven to 425°F.

4 Turn out the risen dough, punch down and knead again. Divide into two and shape into rounds. Place on the baking sheet, and punch hollows in the dough. Trickle over the remaining olive oil and sprinkle with salt.

5 Bake the focaccia for 12–15 minutes until golden brown and cooked. Slide off onto wire racks to cool. Eat slightly warm.

Brown Soda Bread

This is very easy to make – all you have to do is simply mix and bake. Instead of yeast, baking soda and cream of tartar are the rising agents. This is an excellent recipe for those new to bread making.

MAKES ONE 2 LB LOAF
4 cups all-purpose flour
3 cups whole wheat flour
2 tsp salt
1 tbsp baking soda
4 tsp cream of tartar
2 tsp superfine sugar
4 tbsp butter
up to 3¾ cups buttermilk or skimmed milk
extra whole wheat flour, to sprinkle

1 Lightly grease a baking sheet. Preheat the oven to 375°F.

2 Sift all the dry ingredients into a large bowl, tipping any bran from the flour back into the bowl.

3 Rub the butter into the flour mixture, then add enough buttermilk or milk to make a soft dough. You may not need all of it, so add it cautiously.

4 Knead lightly until smooth then transfer to the baking sheet and shape to a large round about 2 in thick.

5 Using the floured handle of a wooden spoon, form a large cross on top of the dough. Sprinkle over a little extra whole wheat flour.

6 Bake for 40–50 minutes until risen and firm. Cool for 5 minutes before transferring to a wire rack to cool further.

Cardamom and Saffron Tea Loaf

An aromatic sweet bread ideal for afternoon tea, or lightly toasted for breakfast. Use the packages of fast action or easy blend yeasts, they make bread making so simple.

MAKES ONE 2 LB LOAF
good pinch saffron strands
3 cups lukewarm milk
2 tbsp butter
8 cups all-purpose flour
2 packages fast action yeast
1½ oz superfine sugar
6 cardamom pods, split open and seeds
    extracted
⅔ cup raisins
2 tbsp honey
1 egg, beaten

1 Crush the saffron into a cup containing a little of the warm milk and leave to infuse for 5 minutes.

2 Rub the butter into the flour then mix in the yeast, sugar and cardamom seeds (these may need rubbing to separate them). Stir in the raisins.

3 Beat the remaining milk with the honey and egg, then mix this into the flour along with the saffron milk and strands, stirring well until a firm dough is formed. You may not need all the milk: it depends on the flour.

4 Turn out the dough and knead it on a lightly floured board for about 5 minutes until smooth.

5 Return the dough to the mixing bowl, cover with oiled plastic wrap and leave in a warm place until doubled in size. This could take between 1–3 hours.

VARIATION

For simplicity, leave out the saffron and cardamom and replace with 2 tsp ground cinnamon.

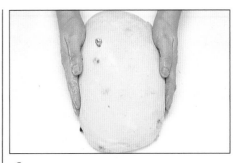

6 Turn the dough out onto a floured board again, punch it down, knead for 3 minutes then shape it into a fat roll and fit it into a greased loaf pan.

7 Cover with a sheet of lightly oiled plastic wrap and stand in a warm place until the dough begins to rise again. Preheat the oven to 400°F.

8 Bake the loaf for 25 minutes until golden brown and firm on top. Turn out of the pan and as it cools brush the top with honey. Slice when cold and spread with butter. It is also good lightly toasted.

Dinner Milk Rolls

Making bread especially for your dinner guests is not only a wonderful gesture, it is also quite easy to do. You can vary the shapes of the rolls too.

MAKES 12–16
4 cups all-purpose flour
2 tsp salt
2 tbsp butter
1 package easy-blend fast action yeast
scant 2 cups lukewarm milk
extra cold milk, to glaze
poppy, sesame and sunflower seeds or sea
    salt flakes, to garnish

1 Sift the flour and salt into a large bowl or food processor. Rub in or blend in the butter, then mix in the yeast.

2 Mix to a firm dough with the milk, adding it cautiously if the dough is a little dry in case you don't need it all.

3 Knead for at least 5 minutes by hand, or for 2 minutes in a food processor. Place in a bowl, cover with oiled plastic wrap and leave to rise until doubled in size.

4 Turn out of the bowl, punch down and knead again, then break off into 12–16 pieces and either roll each one into a round or make into fun shapes.

5 Place on an oiled baking sheet, glaze the tops with extra milk and sprinkle over seeds or sea salt flakes of your choice.

6 Leave to start rising again, while you preheat the oven to 450°F. Bake the rolls for 12 minutes or until golden brown and cooked. Leave to cool on a wire rack. Eat as soon as possible, as homemade bread stales quickly.

Indian Pan-fried Breads

Instead of yeast, this dough uses baking soda as a rising agent. Traditional Indian spices add a tasty bite to the bread.

MAKES ABOUT 24
2 cups whole wheat flour
2 cups all-purpose flour
1 tsp salt
1 tsp sugar
2 tsp baking soda
2 tsp cumin seeds
2 tsp black mustard seeds
1 tsp fennel seeds
1 lb natural yogurt
6 tbsp vegetable ghee or clarified butter
5 tbsp sunflower oil

1 Mix the flours with the salt, sugar, baking soda and spices. Mix to a firm dough with the yogurt, being sure to add the yogurt in gradual amounts, as you may not need it all.

2 If the dough is too dry, add cold water slowly until you achieve the correct consistency. Cover and chill for 2 hours.

3 Divide the dough into 24 pieces and roll each piece out to a thin round. Stack the rounds under a clean dish towel as you roll out the rest.

4 Fry the breads in the hot ghee or butter and oil, starting with a quarter and adding more ghee/butter and oil each time you fry. Drain the breads well on kitchen paper towel and store under the dish towel. Serve with curries and raitas.

Rich Chocolate Cake

A simple all-in-one cake sandwiched with a simple but very delicious ganache icing. It makes a particularly good special-occasion cake.

SERVES 6–8
1 cup self-rising flour
3 tbsp cocoa
1 tsp baking powder
10 tbsp butter, softened, or sunflower margarine
¾ cup superfine sugar
3 eggs, beaten
2 tbsp water
ICING
5 oz dark (plain) chocolate
⅔ cup heavy cream
1 tsp vanilla extract
2 tbsp apricot or raspberry jam

1 Grease and line a deep 8 in round cake pan with waxed paper, and then preheat the oven to 325°F.

2 Put all the cake ingredients into a large bowl or food processor. Beat very well with a wooden spoon or blend in the food processor until the mixture is smooth and creamy.

3 Spoon into the cake pan and bake for about 40–45 minutes or until risen and springy to the touch. Cool upside down on a wire rack for 15 minutes, then turn out and set aside to cool completely.

4 To make the icing, break the chocolate into a heatproof bowl and pour in the cream and vanilla extract. Melt in a microwave on full power for 2–3 minutes, or over a pan of simmering water.

5 Cool the icing, stirring it occasionally and chill lightly until it thickens. Split the cake in half. Spread the jam on one half and half the icing on top of that.

6 Sandwich the two halves together and spread the rest of the icing on top, swirling it attractively or marking it with the tip of a table knife. Decorate as desired with candies or candles – even edible flowers can add a nice touch.

Passion Cake

So called because this is a cake associated with Passion Sunday. The carrots and banana give the cake a rich, moist texture.

SERVES 6–8
1¾ cups self-rising flour
2 tsp baking powder
1 tsp cinnamon
½ tsp fresh nutmeg, grated
10 tbsp butter, softened, or sunflower margarine
¾ cup soft brown sugar
grated rind of 1 lemon
2 eggs, beaten
2 carrots, coarsely grated
1 ripe banana, mashed
¾ cup raisins
½ cup walnuts or pecans, chopped
2 tbsp milk
FROSTING
7 oz cream cheese, softened
1½ oz confectioners' sugar
juice of 1 lemon
grated rind of 1 orange
6–8 walnuts, halved
coffee crystal sugar, to sprinkle

1 Grease and line a deep 8 in cake pan with waxed paper. Preheat the oven to 350°F. Sift the flour, baking powder and spices into a bowl.

2 Using an electric mixer, cream the butter and sugar with the lemon rind until it is light and fluffy, then beat in the eggs. Fold in the flour mixture, then the carrots, banana, raisins, nuts and milk.

3 Spoon the mixture into the prepared pan, level the top and bake for about 1 hour until it is risen and the top is springy to touch. Turn the pan upside down and allow the cake to cool in the pan for 30 minutes. Turn onto a wire rack.

4 When cold, split the cake in half. Cream the cheese with the confectioners' sugar, lemon juice and orange rind, then sandwich the two halves together with half of the frosting.

5 Spread the rest of the frosting on top, swirling it attractively. Decorate with the walnut halves and sprinkle with the coffee crystal sugar.

Yogurt with Apricots and Pistachios

If you allow a thick yogurt to drain overnight, it becomes even thicker and more luscious. Add honeyed apricots and nuts and you have an exotic yet simple dessert.

SERVES 4
1 lb yogurt
⅔ cup no-need-to-soak natural dried apricots, snipped
1 tbsp honey
orange rind, grated
2 tbsp unsalted pistachios, roughly chopped
ground cinnamon

VARIATION

For a simple dessert, strain the fruit, cover with yogurt and sprinkle with brown sugar and a little allspice or cinnamon.

1 Place the yogurt in a fine sieve and allow it to drain overnight in the fridge over a bowl.

2 Discard the whey from the yogurt. Place the apricots in a saucepan, barely cover with water and simmer for just 3 minutes, to soften. Drain and transfer to a bowl, then mix with the honey.

3 Mix the yogurt with the apricots, orange rind and nuts. Spoon into sundae dishes, sprinkle over a little cinnamon and chill.

Fresh Pineapple Salad

Very refreshing, this salad can be prepared ahead. Orange flower water is available from Middle Eastern food stores or good delicatessens.

SERVES 4
1 small ripe pineapple
confectioners' sugar, to taste
1 tbsp orange flower water, or more if liked
good ½ cup fresh dates, pitted and quartered
8 oz fresh strawberries, sliced
few fresh mint sprigs, to serve

1 Cut the skin from the pineapple and, using the tip of a vegetable peeler, remove as many brown 'eyes' as possible. Quarter lengthways, remove the core then slice.

2 Lay the pineapple in a shallow, pretty glass bowl. Sprinkle with sugar and orange flower water.

3 Add the dates and strawberries to the pineapple, cover and chill for a good 2 hours, stirring once or twice. Serve lightly chilled decorated with a few mint sprigs.

Walnut and Raspberry Meringue

Make sure you beat the egg whites stiffly to form a good firm foam for the meringue. When you fold in the nuts the meringue will hold its shape. Assemble this dish just before serving, if at all possible.

SERVES 4–6
3 egg whites
few drops of fresh lemon juice
1 cup superfine sugar
¾ cup walnuts, finely chopped
1 lb fresh raspberries
¾ cup sour cream or heavy cream
few drops vanilla extract
confectioners' sugar, to taste

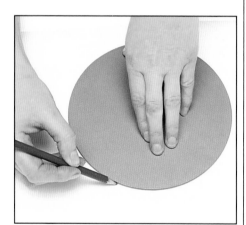

1 Preheat the oven to 325°F. Draw three 8 in circles on non-stick parchment paper. Place the circles on baking sheets.

COOK'S TIP

Don't waste egg whites if you have recipes which call for yolks only. They do freeze very well and can be stored in batches of 3 or 4 whites at a time. In fact, when thawed, frozen egg whites make a much better foam.

2 Whisk the egg whites in a spotlessly clean and grease-free bowl with the few drops of lemon juice. (This gives a more stable foam).

3 When the whites are softly stiff, gradually whisk in the sugar until thick and glossy. Quickly and carefully fold in the nuts.

4 Spread or pipe the mixture onto the three paper circles. Bake for 40–50 minutes until firm and crisp on top. This may have to be done in batches.

5 Cool on a wire rack and peel off the paper. Store in an airtight container until ready to serve.

6 Whip the sour cream or cream with the vanilla and sugar, until the mixture is quite stiff.

7 Reserve a few raspberries for decoration, crush those remaining and mix into the creamy cheese mixture.

8 Spread the fruit cream on the three meringues. Sandwich them together and decorate the top layer with the reserved raspberries.

Rum-Baked Bananas

This is a quick, hot dessert which bakes in just minutes. When cooked, bananas have a really full flavor that is enhanced by rum and orange. Serve this dish with a trickle of cream.

SERVES 4
4 bananas
grated rind and juice of 1 orange
2 tbsp dark rum
¼ cup soft brown sugar (optional)
good pinch of ground ginger
fresh nutmeg, grated
3 tbsp butter

1 Preheat the oven to 350°F. Peel the bananas and then slice them into four large ramekins.

2 Spoon the orange juice and rum over the sliced bananas. Sprinkle over the sugar, if using, orange rind and spices. Dot with butter.

3 Cover the ramekins with small pieces of foil or buttered waxed paper and bake for 15 minutes. Allow to cool slightly before serving with cream or yogurt.

Muesli Bars

Instead of buying expensive crunchy oat bars, bake your own. They are much nicer and really quite easy to make. Use muesli with no added sugar for the bars.

MAKES 12–16
4 cups muesli
5 tbsp sunflower oil
5 tbsp honey
1 tsp mixed spice
1 egg, beaten
1½ oz dark brown sugar (optional)

COOK'S TIP

To make your own muesli, buy bags of flaked grains and oats from your local health food store. As these will make a large amount, you need to make sure you eat a lot of muesli! Choose jumbo rolled oats, barley flakes and wheat flakes, then add a selection of seeds, dried fruits and nuts.

1 Preheat the oven to 325°F. Grease and line a shallow baking pan measuring about 7 × 11 in.

2 Mix all the ingredients together and spoon into the pan, patting the mixture until it is level.

3 Bake for 30–35 minutes until light brown round the edges. Remove, cool slightly then mark into 12–16 pieces.

4 Cool completely, turn out onto a wire rack and break into the marked pieces. Store in an airtight container.

Oatmeal and Date Brownies

These brownies are marvelous for special brunches or as a tea time treat. The secret of chewy, moist brownies is not to overcook them.

MAKES 16
5 oz dark (plain) chocolate
4 tbsp butter
¾ cup rolled oats
3 tbsp wheat germ
⅓ cup milk powder
½ tsp baking powder
½ tsp salt
½ cup walnuts, chopped
⅓ cup dates, chopped
¼ cup dark brown sugar
1 tsp vanilla extract
2 eggs, beaten

1 Break the chocolate into a heatproof bowl and add the butter. Melt it either in a microwave on full power for 2 minutes, stirring once, or in a pan over very gently simmering water.

2 Cool the chocolate, stirring it occasionally. Grease and line an 8 in square cake pan with waxed paper, then preheat the oven to 350°F.

3 Combine all the dry ingredients together in a bowl then beat in the melted chocolate, vanilla and eggs.

4 Pour the mixture into the prepared cake pan, level the top and bake for about 20–25 minutes until it is firm around the edges yet still soft in the center.

5 Cool the brownies in the pan, then chill. When they are more solid, turn them out of the pan and cut into 16 squares. Store in an airtight container.

COOK'S TIP

These make a marvelous lunch box or picnic snack, and if you store them for a day or two before eating they will become more moist and even more chewy.

Cut-and-Come-Again Fruit Cake

A rich fruit cake keeps well for quite some time so it is ideal to have one on hand for when you feel like a slice of something sweet or when guests drop in unexpectedly.

SERVES 8–10
2 sticks butter, softened, or sunflower
  margarine
1 cup soft brown sugar
4 eggs, beaten
1 tbsp black molasses
3 cups all-purpose flour
1 tsp cinnamon
3 tbsp milk
2 lb dried mixed fruit (e.g. raisins,
  currants, cherries)
½ cup flaked almonds
grated rind of 1 lemon
a few blanched almond halves (optional)
a little milk, to glaze (optional)
2 tbsp brandy or rum (optional)

1 Preheat the oven to 275°F. Grease and line a deep 8 in cake pan with doubled waxed paper.

2 Cream the butter or margarine and sugar until light and fluffy. Beat in the eggs with the molasses and stir into the creamed mixture.

3 Sift the flour and spice and fold this into the mixture, alternating it with the milk. Stir in the dried fruit, almonds and lemon rind.

4 Spoon the mixture into the prepared pan. If liked, dip the almond halves in a little milk and arrange them on top.

5 Bake on a shelf one position below the center of the oven for about 3 hours. When cooked, the top of the cake will feel quite firm and a skewer inserted into the center will come out clean.

6 Allow the cake to cool for 10 minutes then, if using the brandy or rum, make small holes in the top of the cake with a thin skewer. Slowly pour the liquor over the cake.

7 Allow the cake to cool completely in the pan, then turn it out and remove the paper. Wrap it in clean waxed paper and foil or store in an airtight container for one week before cutting.

Thai Rice Cake

A celebration gâteau made from fragrant Thai rice covered with a tangy cream icing. Top with fresh berry fruits or pipe on a greeting in melted chocolate. This is a good cake to serve to those with a gluten allergy as it is flour free.

SERVES 8–10
1¼ cups Thai fragrant or Jasmine rice
4½ cups milk
¾ cup superfine sugar
6 cardamom pods, crushed open
2 bay leaves
1¼ cups whipping cream
6 eggs, separated
TOPPING
1¼ cups heavy cream
7 oz cream cheese
1 tsp vanilla extract
grated rind of 1 lemon
1½ oz superfine sugar
soft berry fruits and sliced star or kiwi
    fruits, to decorate

1 Grease and line a deep 10 in round cake pan. Boil the rice in unsalted water for 3 minutes then drain.

2 Return the rice to the pan with the milk, sugar, cardamom and bay leaves. Bring to a boil, then lower the heat and simmer the mixture for 20 minutes, stirring it occasionally.

3 Allow the mixture to cool, then remove the bay leaves and any cardamom husks. Turn the mixture into a bowl. Beat in the cream and then the egg yolks. Preheat the oven to 350°F.

VARIATION

If you prefer something simpler, turn the cake out and top with sliced fruits or a lovely tumble of berries and pitted cherries. Serve the topping separately, thinning it down slightly with a little milk.

4 Whisk the egg whites until they are softly stiff and fold into the rice mixture. Spoon into the prepared pan and bake for 45–50 minutes until risen and golden brown. The center should be slightly wobbly – it will firm up as it cools.

5 Chill overnight in the pan. Turn out on to a serving plate. Whip the heavy cream until stiff then mix in the cream cheese, vanilla, lemon rind and sugar.

6 Cover the top and sides of the cake with the cream, swirling it attractively. Decorate with soft berry fruits and sliced star or kiwi fruits.

Apple and Apricot Crumble

Lightly cook the fruit base first for the best results. That way you'll get a delicious contrast between soft fruit and crunchy topping.

SERVES 4—6
1 × 15 oz can apricot halves in natural juice
1 lb cooking apples, peeled and sliced
granulated sugar, to taste (optional)
grated rind of 1 orange
fresh nutmeg, grated
TOPPING
1¾ cups all-purpose flour
½ cup rolled oats
10 tbsp butter or sunflower margarine
¼ cup soft brown sugar
light brown sugar, to sprinkle

1 Preheat the oven to 375°F. Drain the apricot halves, reserving a little of the natural juice.

2 Put the apples into a saucepan with a little of the reserved apricot juice and sugar to taste. Simmer for just 5 minutes to cook the fruit lightly.

3 Transfer the apples into an ovenproof pie dish and stir in the apricots, orange rind and nutmeg to taste.

4 Rub the flour, oats and butter or margarine together until they form fine crumbs. (You can use a food processor if you prefer.) Mix in the soft brown sugar.

5 Scatter the crumble over the fruit, spreading it evenly. Sprinkle with a little brown sugar. Bake for about 30 minutes until golden and crisp on top. Allow to cool slightly before serving.

French Apple Cake

With its moist texture and fruity flavor, this cake is ideal to serve as a dessert accompanied by a little cream or yogurt.

SERVES 6–8
1 lb cooking apples or tart dessert apples, cored and chopped
1 cup self-rising flour
1 tsp baking powder
⅔ cup superfine sugar
6 tbsp milk
4 tbsp butter, melted
3 eggs
1 tsp fresh nutmeg, grated
TOPPING
6 tbsp butter, softened, or sunflower margarine
½ cup superfine sugar
1 tsp vanilla extract
sifted confectioners' sugar, to dust

1 Preheat the oven to 325°F. Grease and line the base of a deep 9 in round cake pan with waxed paper.

2 Put the chopped apples into the base of the cake pan.

3 Put all the remaining cake ingredients, except 1 egg, into a bowl or food processor. Beat to a smooth batter.

4 Pour the batter over the apples in the pan, level the top then bake for 40–45 minutes until lightly golden.

5 Meanwhile, cream the topping ingredients together with the remaining egg. Remove the cake from the oven and spoon over the topping.

6 Return the cake to the oven for a further 20–25 minutes until it is golden brown. Cool the cake in the pan, then turn it out and finish with a light dusting of confectioners' sugar.

VARIATION

We don't use fresh fruit very often in cake mixtures, which is a pity as it gives a delightful flavor. Try adding finely chopped pears or pineapple, or even raspberries.

Halva

The Greeks love home made halva which they cook in a saucepan with semolina, olive oil, sugar, honey and almonds. You can either eat it warm, or allow it to set and cut it into slices or squares.

MAKES 12–16 PIECES
2 cups granulated sugar
4½ cups water
2 cinnamon sticks
1 cup olive oil
3 cups semolina
¾ cup blanched almonds, 6–8 halved, the rest chopped
½ cup honey
ground cinnamon, to serve

1 Reserve 4 tbsp sugar and dissolve the rest in the water over a gentle heat, stirring from time to time.

2 Add the cinnamon sticks, bring to a boil then simmer for 5 minutes. Cool and remove the cinnamon sticks.

3 Heat the olive oil in a large heavy-based saucepan and, when it is quite hot, stir in the semolina. Cook, stirring occasionally, until it turns a golden brown, then add the chopped almonds and cook for a further minute or so.

4 Keep the heat low and stir in the syrup, taking care as the semolina may spit. Bring the mixture to a boil, stirring it constantly. When it is just smooth, remove the pan from the heat and stir in the honey.

5 Cool slightly and mix in the reserved sugar. Pour the halva into a greased and lined shallow pan, pat it down and mark into squares.

6 Sprinkle the halva lightly with ground cinnamon and fix one almond half on each square. When set, cut up and serve.

Rice Condé Sundae

Cook a rice pudding on top of the stove instead of in the oven for a light creamy texture which is particularly good served cold topped with fruits, toasted nuts and even a trickle of hot chocolate sauce.

SERVES 4
⅓ cup pudding rice
2½ cups milk
1 tsp vanilla extract
½ tsp ground cinnamon
1½ oz granulated sugar
TO SERVE
Choose from: strawberries, raspberries or
    blueberries
chocolate sauce
flaked toasted almonds

1 Put the rice, milk, vanilla extract, cinnamon and sugar into a medium-sized saucepan. Bring to a boil, stirring constantly, and then turn down the heat to a gentle simmer.

2 Cook the rice for about 30–40 minutes, stirring occasionally. Add extra milk if it reduces down too quickly.

3 Make sure the grains are soft, then remove the pan from the heat and allow the rice to cool, stirring it occasionally. When cold, chill the rice in the refrigerator.

4 Just before serving, stir the rice and spoon into four sundae dishes. Top with fruits, chocolate sauce and almonds.

VARIATION

Milk puddings are at last enjoying something of a comeback in popularity. Instead of simple pudding rice try using a Thai fragrant or Jasmine rice for a delicious natural flavor. For a firmer texture, an Italian Arborio rice makes a good pudding too.

There's no need to use a lot of high-fat milk or cream either. A pudding made with low fat or even fat-free milk can be just as nice and is much more healthy.

Three-fruits Compôte

Mixing dried fruits with fresh ones makes a good combination, especially if flavored delicately with a little orange flower water. A melon-ball scoop gives the compôte a classy touch, but you could simply chop the melon into cubes.

SERVES 6
1 cup no-need-to-soak dried apricots
1 small ripe pineapple
1 small ripe melon
1 tbsp orange flower water

1 Put the apricots into a saucepan with ½ pint water. Bring to a boil, then simmer for 5 minutes. Leave to cool.

2 Peel and quarter the pineapple then cut the core from each quarter and discard. Cut the flesh into chunks.

3 Seed the melon and scoop balls from the flesh. Save any juices which fall from the fruits and tip them into the apricots.

4 Stir in the orange flower water and mix all the fruits together. Pour into an attractive serving dish and chill lightly before serving.

VARIATION

A good fruit salad needn't be a boring mixture of multi-colored fruits swimming in sweet syrup. Instead of the usual apple, orange and grape type of salad, give it a theme, such as red berry fruits or a variety of sliced green fruits – even a dish of just one fruit nicely prepared and sprinkled lightly with some sugar and fresh lemon juice can look beautiful and tastes delicious. Do not use more than three fruits in a salad so that the flavors remain distinct.

Red Berry Tart with Lemon Cream Filling

Just right for warm summer days, this tart is best filled just before serving so the pastry remains mouth-wateringly crisp. Select a range of red berry fruits such as strawberries, raspberries or red currants.

SERVES 6–8
1¼ cups all-purpose flour
¼ cup cornstarch
1½ oz confectioners' sugar
8 tbsp butter
1 tsp vanilla extract
2 egg yolks, beaten
FILLING
7 oz cream cheese, softened
3 tbsp lemon curd
grated rind and juice of 1 lemon
confectioners' sugar, to sweeten (optional)
8 oz mixed red berry fruits
3 tbsp red currant jelly

1 Sift the flour, cornstarch and confectioners' sugar together, then rub in the butter until the mixture resembles bread crumbs.

2 Beat the vanilla into the egg yolks, then mix into the crumbs to make a firm dough, adding cold water if necessary.

3 Roll out and line a 9 in round pie pan, pressing the dough well up the sides after trimming. Prick the base of the tart with a fork and allow it to rest in the refrigerator for 30 minutes.

4 Preheat the oven to 400°F. Line the tart with waxed paper and baking beans. Place the pan on a baking sheet and bake for 20 minutes, removing the paper and beans for the last 5 minutes. When cooked, cool and remove the pastry shell from the pie pan.

VARIATION

There are all sorts of delightful variations to this recipe. For instance, leave out the red currant jelly and sprinkle lightly with confectioners' sugar or decorate with fresh mint leaves. Alternatively, top with sliced kiwi fruits.

5 Cream the cheese, lemon curd and lemon rind and juice, adding a little confectioners' sugar to sweeten, if you wish. Spread the mixture into the tart.

6 Top the tart with the fruits. Warm the red currant jelly and trickle it over the fruits just before serving.

Honey and Lemon Spicy Mincemeat

Like Christmas Pudding, mincemeat is best made a few weeks ahead to allow the flavors to mature. This mixture is lighter than most traditional recipes.

MAKES 3 LB
1 cup vegetarian shredded suet
1½ cups currants
1 large cooking apple, coarsely grated
grated rind of 2 lemons
grated rind and juice of 1 orange
¾ cup no-need-to-soak prunes, chopped
¾ cup pitted dates, chopped
1 cup raisins
1¼ cups sultanas
1 cup flaked almonds
6 tbsp honey
4 tbsp brandy or rum
1 tsp cinnamon
½ tsp ground cloves or allspice

1 Mix all the ingredients together well in a large mixing bowl. Cover and store in a cool place for two days, stirring the mixture occasionally.

2 Sterilize clean jam jars by placing them in a warm oven for 30 minutes. Cool, then fill with mincemeat, and seal with wax discs and screw tops. Label and store until required.

Cinnamon and Molasses Cookies

The smell of home made cookies baking is bettered only by their wonderful taste! These cookies are slightly sticky, spicy and nutty.

MAKES 24
2 tbsp black molasses
4 tbsp butter or margarine
1 cup all-purpose flour
¼ tsp baking soda
½ tsp ground ginger
1 tsp ground cinnamon
¼ cup soft brown sugar
1 tbsp ground almonds or hazelnuts
1 egg yolk
1 cup confectioners' sugar, sifted

1 Heat the molasses and butter or margarine until they just begin to melt.

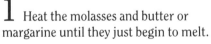

2 Sift the flour into a large bowl with the baking soda and spices, then stir in the sugar and almonds or nuts.

3 Beat the molasses mixture briskly into the bowl together with the egg yolk and draw the ingredients together to form a firm but soft dough.

4 Roll the dough out on a lightly floured surface to a ¼ in thickness and stamp out shapes, such as stars, hearts or circles. Re-roll the trimmings for more shapes. Place on a very lightly greased baking sheet and chill for 15 minutes.

5 Meanwhile, preheat the oven to 375°F. Prick the cookies lightly all over with a fork and bake them for 12–15 minutes until they are just firm. Cool on wire trays to crisp up.

6 To decorate, mix the confectioners' sugar with a little lukewarm water to make it slightly runny, then drizzle it over the cookies on the wire tray.

Mince Pies with Orange Cinnamon Pastry

Home made mince pies are so much nicer than store-bought, especially with a flavorsome pastry.

MAKES 18
2 cups all-purpose flour
1½ oz confectioners' sugar, plus a little extra for dusting
2 tsp ground cinnamon
10 tbsp butter
grated rind of 1 orange
4 tbsp ice cold water
1½ cups vegetarian mincemeat
1 beaten egg, to glaze

1 Sift together the flour, sugar and cinnamon, then rub in the butter until it forms crumbs. (This can be done in a food processor.) Stir in the grated orange rind.

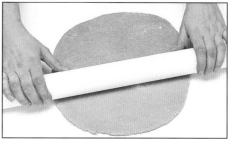

2 Mix to a firm dough with the ice cold water. Knead lightly, then roll out to a ¼ in thickness.

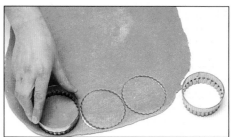

3 Using a 2½ in round cutter, cut out 18 circles, re-rolling as necessary. Then cut out 18 circles with a 2 in cutter. If liked, cut out little shapes from the centers of the smaller circles.

4 Line two muffin pans with the 18 larger circles – they will fill one and a half pans. Spoon a small spoonful of mincemeat into each pastry case and top with the smaller pastry circles, pressing the edges lightly together to seal.

5 Glaze the tops of the pies with egg and leave to rest in the refrigerator for approximately 30 minutes. Preheat the oven to 400°F.

6 Bake the pies for 15–20 minutes until they are golden brown. Remove them to wire racks to cool. Serve just warm and dusted with confectioners' sugar.

Christmas Pudding

If possible, try to make your puddings at least one month before Christmas for the flavors to develop and mature. Dried prunes and apricots add an unusual texture and delicious flavor to this recipe.

MAKES TWO 2 PINT PUDDINGS
5 cups fresh white bread crumbs
2 cups shredded vegetarian suet or ice cold butter, coarsely grated
1 cup all-purpose flour
1 cup soft brown sugar
2 tsp ground mixed spice
2½ cups currants
2½ cups raisins
1¾ cups sultanas
1 cup pitted no-need-to-soak prunes, chopped
¾ cup no-need-to-soak dried apricots, chopped
¾ cup candied citrus peel, chopped
¾ cup glacé cherries, washed and chopped
rind of 1 large lemon, grated
4 eggs, beaten
2 tbsp black molasses
⅔ cup beer or milk
4 tbsp brandy or rum

1 Grease two 2 pint Pyrex bowls and then line the base of each with small discs of waxed paper.

2 Mix all the ingredients together well. If you intend to put lucky coins or tokens in the mixture, boil them first to ensure they are clean and wrap them in foil.

3 Pack the mixture into the two bowls, pushing it down lightly.

4 Cover each pudding with greased waxed paper and a double thickness of foil. Secure the foil round the rim with lengths of kitchen string.

5 Place two old china saucers in the base of two large saucepans. Stand the basins on the saucers, pour boiling water to come two thirds of the way up and boil gently for about 6 hours, checking the water level regularly and topping it up with more boiling water.

6 When cooked, cool the puddings, remove the foil and paper then re-cover to store. On Christmas Day, re-boil for about 2 hours and serve with brandy butter and cream or custard.

Index